THE SPIRITUAL FOUNDATION OF MORALITY

THE SPIRITUAL FOUNDATION OF MORALITY

Francis of Assisi and the Christ Impulse

THREE LECTURES
BY
RUDOLF STEINER

Norrköping, Sweden
May 28–30, 1912

TRANSLATED FROM THE GERMAN
BY
MALCOLM IAN GARDNER

 ANTHROPOSOPHIC PRESS

This volume is a translation of *Theosophische Moral* (3rd edition, 1994, published as part of vol. 155 of the *Rudolf Steiner Gesamtausgabe*, Rudolf Steiner Verlag, Dornach, Switzerland). Translation, introduction, and notes by Malcolm Ian Gardner.

Copyright © 1995 by Anthroposophic Press
Translator's Introduction © 1995 by Malcolm Ian Gardner

Published by Anthroposophic Press
RR 4 Box 94 A-1, Hudson, NY 12534

Library of Congress Cataloging-in-Publication Data

Steiner, Rudolf, 1861–1925.
  [Theosophische Moral. English]
  The spiritual foundation of morality : Francis of Assisi and the
Christ impulse / Rudolf Steiner : translated by Malcolm Ian Gardner.
    p.   cm.
  ISBN 0-88010-425-2
  1. Anthroposophy. 2. Spiritual life. 3. Francis of Assisi,
Saint, 1182–1226. I. Title.
  BP595. S894T4813   1995
  299'.934—cd20   95-22292
                                                               CIP

10 9 8 7 6 5 4 3 2 1

CONTENTS

TRANSLATOR'S INTRODUCTION

In these times of moral breakdown, when the social fabric is torn and frayed, where can our souls find strength? The fundamental premise of the three lectures presented here is twofold: that the soul of the human being needs nourishment, and that in modern times this nourishment must come through consciously acquired knowledge. Slogans and exhortations do not nourish the soul; they may make it more obedient for a while, but they cannot make it stronger or more moral. What the soul needs, however, is not any kind of technical or manipulative knowledge, but true insight, true *wisdom*. Through its very beauty, wisdom nourishes, enlarges and uplifts the soul, and allows it to become mysteriously filled with the power of compassion and moral integrity. It was Rudolf Steiner's claim that the wisdom of the ancients was a reflection of the divine world order, and that in the body of knowledge known as *theosophy*, or later as *anthroposophy*, a portion of this divine world order now exists in a form accessible to our modern intellectual age.

Among modern spiritual teachers, Rudolf Steiner (1861–1925) occupies a very unique position. He was not only a highly gifted clairvoyant, he was also a trained and exceptionally clear thinker who approached the spiritual worlds with the rigor of a scientist.[1] His accounts of the spiritual worlds and their relationship to the physical world are characteristically detailed and concrete. In the first of the lectures that follow, he approaches the subject of morality through a series of concrete historical examples, culminating with the life of St. Francis of Assisi. In the second lecture he discloses the dramatic spiritual background of these examples, and in the last lecture he shows why particular moral virtues have changed through history and how they fit into a grand evolutionary pattern. All this is done with exquisite tactfulness and artistry, so that the facts and the wisdom of the world speak for themselves.

•••••

THE TACTFULNESS WITH which Rudolf Steiner delivered these lectures is all the more noteworthy in light of their historical context. At the time (1912), Steiner was still General Secretary of the German Section of the Theosophical Society. In this capacity he traveled around Europe, primarily but not exclusively in the German-speaking countries, giving lectures based on his own spiritual research. Indeed, when he had first accepted the post of Secretary in 1901, he had made it a condition that he be allowed to speak with complete freedom, and in the ensuing decade he had given theosophy a more scientific and universal character than had previously been customary in the Theosophical Society. Above all he had emphasized the uniqueness and universality of the Christ and the Mystery of Golgotha, and this had caused considerable

---

1.   For biographical details, see *Rudolf Steiner: An Autobiography* (Blauvelt, N.Y.: Rudolf Steiner Publ., 1977), or A. P. Shepherd, *Scientist of the Invisible* (New York: Inner Traditions, 1983). Steiner also referred to his work as "spiritual science" or "occult science."

consternation because in traditional theosophy—deriving largely from H. P. Blavatsky—pre-eminence had always been granted to Eastern religious figures such as the Buddha. Steiner, however, stressed that while the great significance of the Buddha lay in his teaching, the great significance of the Christ lay in his unique, sacrificial deed, which had imparted a macrocosmic spiritual impulse to the earth and to all of humanity.[2]

It thus came about that although Steiner's brand of theosophy was much appreciated in the German Section, in other parts of the Theosophical Society an undercurrent of resentment gradually developed. This current gathered momentum after 1910 with the endorsement by the leadership of the Society of a young boy in India as the vehicle for an imminent reincarnation of the "World Teacher" (who it was claimed had previously manifested through Jesus). To Steiner, this was a materialistic perversion of the true spiritual facts and he refused to support the preparatory activities. He did not break with the Society but instead redoubled his effort to explain the true situation. This effort was partially thwarted by the last-minute cancellation of the 1911 Congress of the Theosophical Society. Finally, in the autumn of 1912, a group of members within the German Section realized that no reconciliation was possible and took the initiative to form a separate Society, which they asked Steiner to lead (and to name). By early 1913, most of the members of the German Section had joined the newly constituted Anthroposophical Society.[3]

---

2.   See, for example, Steiner's book *Christianity as Mystical Fact and the Mysteries of Antiquity* (Blauvelt, N.Y.: Steinerbooks, 1961), and his lecture of May 5, 1912, in *The Festivals and Their Meaning* (London: Rudolf Steiner Press, 1981), lec. 11.

3.   Steiner himself preferred to become an independent advisor to the Anthroposophical Society; he did not become a member until he took on the

It is evident from the foregoing that when the present lectures were given in Norrköping, Sweden, in May 1912, tensions within the Theosophical Society were already quite high. In fact, these lectures to the members were directly preceded by the annual general meeting of the Scandinavian Section of the Theosophical Society on May 26 and 27 (Whitsunday and Whitmonday). Moreover, it is evident from the opening sentence of Steiner's first lecture that he was not responding to a request, but that it was his own choice to speak on the topic of morality. And yet, hardly a trace of the Society's difficulties are to be found in the lectures themselves. At most one may detect a certain emphasis on the virtue of truthfulness. Thus, although he clearly wished to stimulate some soul-searching on the part of the members, in his lectures he did not focus on the Society's problems, but rather on its potential. In this tactfulness we may recognize the scrupulous respect he had for the members' individual freedom.

•••••

THE THEME OF FREEDOM and morality runs through Steiner's life like a red thread. From his early period as a literary scholar and philosopher there is his classic book *The Philosophy of Freedom*.[4] After his emergence as a spiritual teacher there are the many exercises he described for developing specific virtues as a

---

Presidency in 1923. For details on the birth of the Anthroposophical Society, see G. Wachsmuth, *The Life and Work of Rudolf Steiner* (New York: Whittier Books, 1955). The Indian boy was Jiddu Krishnamurti; he renounced his Messianic role in 1929.

4.   Published in 1894 as *Die Philosophie der Freiheit*; also translated into English as *The Philosophy of Spiritual Activity* and, most recently, as *Intuitive Thinking as a Spiritual Path* (Hudson, N.Y.: Anthroposophic Press, 1995).

foundation for spiritual knowledge.[5] Then toward the end of his life there is his great emphasis on the spiritual being known as Michaël, the spirit of freedom and courage.[6] And still, this brief lecture series in Norrköping stands out as his most direct and concentrated discussion of morality as such. It is also worth noting that one of the main themes here—the significance of human virtues for the Christ's own development—was never mentioned by him again.[7]

The Easter preceding these Whitsun lectures was marked by another unique event in Steiner's career: the publication of his extraordinary *Calendar of the Soul* (*Seelenkalendar*).[8] In this Calendar the fifty-two weeks of the year are accompanied by a poem of fifty-two verses, which portray a series of soul processes. In his brief foreword, Steiner states that by meditating on these verses, one can come to recognize the cycle of the seasons as a source of self-knowledge, as the archetype of one's own soul-life. In other words, the harmonious wisdom inherent in this archetype can have an ethical effect on the soul of the meditant. Indeed, in ancient times the natural seasons were experienced as the source of specific moral impulses, which later became known as the four Platonic

---

5.   See especially his book *Wie erlangt man Erkenntnisse der höheren Welten?*, first published serially in 1904–05. Translated into English as *Knowledge of the Higher Worlds and Its Attainment* and as *How to Know Higher Worlds* (Hudson, N.Y.: Anthroposophic Press, 1994).

6.   See, for example, the collection *The Archangel Michael: His Mission and Ours* (Hudson, N.Y.: Anthroposophic Press, 1994).

7.   Furthermore, his first explicit mention of it came only three weeks earlier, on May 8 in Berlin (he then mentioned it again on May 14 in Cologne).

8.   Numerous translations of these verses exist.

(cardinal) virtues.[9] The *Calendar of the Soul* thus forms a beautiful backdrop to the lectures in Norrköping; implicit in both is the moral relationship of the human being as microcosm to the being of the macrocosm.

Although St. Francis of Assisi figures prominently in the Norrköping lectures, Steiner did not mention Francis' strong relationship to nature until his next lecture series, held in Christiania (Oslo), Norway (June 2–12). There he described how it was St. Francis' "mysticism of the heart" that led him to address the sun and the moon, the wind and the water, and all the creatures of nature as "brother" and "sister." His rapport with nature was based on feeling, and was enhanced by the fact that thinking was largely by-passed.[10] Elsewhere Steiner emphasizes, however, that in modern times our rapport with nature must become more conscious, that we must learn to "think with the heart." This is now possible, he says, because of the spiritual help of the being of Michaël, who is the messenger of Christ in the present age.[11]

· · · · ·

READERS PREVIOUSLY unacquainted with Rudolf Steiner's work may be surprised by the way he blends Christianity with seemingly Eastern ideas of reincarnation and karma. In Steiner's hands,

---

9.   See his lecture of Apr. 8, 1923, in *The Cycle of the Year* (Spring Valley, N.Y.: Anthroposophic Press, 1984), lec. 5 (misdated Apr. 4).

10.   See Steiner: June 6, 1912, *Man in the Light of Occultism, Theosophy and Philosophy* (London: Rudolf Steiner Press, 1964), lec. 4.

11.   See Steiner: Mar. 29, 1910, *Microcosm and Macrocosm* (London: Rudolf Steiner Press, 1985), lec. 9; and "At the Dawn of the Michael Age," *Anthroposophical Leading Thoughts* (London: Rudolf Steiner Press, 1973). See also his four lectures from autumn 1923 entitled *Michaelmas and the Soul-Forces of Man* (Spring Valley, N.Y.: Anthroposophic Press, 1946).

however, conventional notions about these subjects are completely transformed; East and West are shown to be necessary counterparts. Steiner explains that during the epoch of Christ's appearance on earth, humanity needed to forget the glories of the spiritual world and learn to love the earthly world. Two millennia later, however, this lesson has been learned and the ancient concepts of reincarnation and karma can and must be reintroduced.[12] Yet they are no longer exactly the same; in their Christian form they no longer refer merely to a path of individual redemption, but to a process wherein the redemptive deeds of each individual are interwoven and contribute to the redemption of all.[13]

New readers may also be somewhat puzzled by Steiner's frequent references to the "Christ Impulse." This is not simply a nebulous term for the spread of Christianity; for Steiner this is a spiritual reality—in fact, as he says in the third lecture, it is the *most* real impulse in world evolution. It is the divine, macrocosmic power that first united with the soul of the man Jesus at the Baptism, and then at the Crucifixion passed over into the soul of humanity, the soul of the planet. As such, the Christ Impulse brings objective redemption to the bodies of all human beings, irrespective of individual belief or knowledge. On the other hand, insofar as the individual souls freely strive to comprehend and accept the Christ Impulse, these souls become filled to overflowing with the impulse of love and self-sacrifice; they become the

---

12. See Steiner: Oct. 3, 1905, *Foundations of Esotericism* (London: Rudolf Steiner Press, 1982), lec. 8. Steiner indicates that in future people will naturally begin to remember their previous lives, but if they are unprepared, this will be a frightening experience (May 1, 1913, *Occult Science and Occult Development* [London: Rudolf Steiner Press, 1966], lec. 1).

13. See Steiner: Oct. 14, 1911, *From Jesus to Christ* (London: Rudolf Steiner Press, 1973), lec. 10.

building stones for a new social order, the fibers for a new social fabric. This individual comprehension of the Christ Impulse is described by Steiner as the gift of the Holy Spirit, the direct reception of which is celebrated at Whitsun.[14] The Holy Spirit's gift of wisdom is also received indirectly through religious traditions as well as through theosophy or anthroposophy. These nourish the soul's moral forces of faith, love and hope, thus preparing it to become a direct recipient and instrument of divine grace.[15]

· · · · ·

ALTHOUGH THE WORD "theosophy" is retained in the present translation, it should be understood here as being equivalent to "anthroposophy," a term which Steiner said "expressed even better" what he wished to bring.[16] Steiner once likened *theosophy* to the view from the top of a mountain, *anthroposophy* to the view from the middle elevations, and *anthropology* to the view from the base of the mountain.[17] Steiner wished not only to unite the overview with

---

14. See Steiner: May 7 & 17, 1923, *The Festivals and Their Meaning* (London: Rudolf Steiner Press, 1981), lecs. 17 & 19.

15. See Steiner: May 31, 1908, *The Gospel of John* (Spring Valley, N.Y.: Anthroposophic Press, 1962), lec. 12; and Lecture Three here.

16. See Steiner's lecture at the first annual meeting of the Anthroposophical Society, February 3, 1913 ("Das Wesen der Anthroposophie"), in *Schicksalszeichen auf dem Entwicklungswege der Anthroposophischen Gesellschaft* (Dornach, Switzerland: Rudolf Steiner Verlag, 1943). Steiner used the term "anthroposophy" outside the Theosophical Society as early as 1902. From October 1902 to April 1903 he gave a course of twenty-seven lectures to a literary club in Berlin; its full title was: "From Zarathustra to Nietzsche. The Evolution of Humanity as Shown in the World Conceptions from the Earliest Oriental Ages down to the Present Time, or Anthroposophy." (No transcript exists.)

17. See Steiner: Oct. 23, 1909, *The Wisdom of Man, of the Soul, and of the Spirit* (New York: Anthroposophic Press 1971), lec. 1.

the details, but also to transform passively received divine wisdom into actively achieved human wisdom.

In this translation the attempt has been made to preserve the freshness and rhythm of Steiner's spoken style. Steiner did not lecture from notes; the German text of these lectures is based on a stenogram by an unknown stenographer. We can be grateful for the high quality of this stenogram, though it probably does not represent an absolutely verbatim report.

Since Steiner gave these lectures to an audience already familiar with his work, he could go far deeper into the subject than would have been possible had he been lecturing to the general public. In the notes to this translation, an attempt has been made to provide or indicate some of the background his original audience may have had. In addition, certain clarifying remarks or references from his subsequent work have also been included. Even with these aids, however, particular questions and riddles are sure to remain. May they serve as a stimulus for the reader's own reflection and active meditation.

THREE LECTURES
BY
RUDOLF STEINER

Norrköping, Sweden

May 28–30, 1912

LECTURE ONE

May 28, 1912

In accordance with a certain impulse of mine, about which we may be able to speak further, we will be taking up in the coming days one of the most important and vital areas of theosophical study.[1] We are indeed often reproached for wanting to study the human being's connection with broad developments in the spiritual cosmos, for wishing to consider far-distant events of the past and far-reaching perspectives of the future while almost completely disregarding the realm that is nearest us—the realm of human morals and human ethics. It is quite true that this realm of human morals must be regarded as one of the most essential, but it must also be said that we feel able to approach this subject only with the greatest reverence and respect, particularly if we experience the full significance of the theosophical conception of life. We realize that it will touch us as closely as anything can—if it is to be considered in the right way—and that it therefore calls for the most serious and worthy preparation.

The reproach that is made against us could perhaps be expressed in the following manner: What is the use of making deep studies of the universe? Why talk about numerous reincarnations, or the complicated conditions of karma, when surely the most important thing in life is what was repeatedly said by a certain wise man to his followers after he had attained the summit of a rich life of wisdom, indeed, after he had grown so weak and ill that he had to be carried. "Children, love one another!"—these words were uttered by John the Evangelist when he was a very old man, and it has often been said that these four words contain the essence of the deepest moral wisdom. And so, many might ask: What more is needed if goodness, if sublime moral ideals, can be fulfilled so simply, as implied by these words of John the Evangelist?[2]

Something is overlooked when the fact of the importance of morality leads people to believe that it is sufficient to know that they should love one another. What is overlooked is that he who uttered these words did so at the close of a rich life of wisdom, a life which included the writing of the most profound and important of the Gospels. He who uttered these words acquired the right to do so only at the end of this rich life of wisdom. He who has lived a life such as this is justified in distilling the deep wisdom contained in the Gospel of St. John into the words just spoken, words which may then also flow out of unfathomable depths of soul into the depths of other hearts and souls. He who is not in such a position, however, must first go deeply into the secret foundations of the world and thereby earn the right to express the highest moral truths in such a simple manner.

The oft-repeated saying—"When two persons say the same thing, it is not the same"—may be trivial, but it is especially valid in this case. When someone who simply refuses to know or understand anything of the mysteries of the world says, "It is really quite simple to describe the highest moral life," and then uses the words, "Children, love one another," this is quite different from the Evangelist John's saying these words. For this reason, someone who understands these words of John ought to draw from them a quite different conclusion than is usually drawn. The conclusion should be that one has first of all to be silent about such profoundly significant words, and that they may be uttered only if one has gone through the necessary preparation and reached the necessary maturity.

But now that we have made this statement—which will certainly have struck a deep chord with some of you—something quite different will come to mind, something of profound importance. You will say to yourself: "It may be true that the deepest significance of moral principles can be understood only at the end of the path of wisdom, but despite this they are used all the time. How would it be possible to foster any kind of moral community or social endeavor, if one had to wait for knowledge of the highest ethical principles until the end of the path of wisdom? Morality is what is most necessary for human social life; yet here it is asserted that moral principles can be acquired only at the culmination of a long striving for wisdom." At this point, some might say that if this were so they would begin to doubt the wise arrangement of the world—if what is needed most could be gained only at the conclusion of human striving.

The answer to what has just been outlined is amply given by life itself. You need only compare two cases—which are no doubt well known to you in one form or another—and you will at once perceive that both assertions can be correct: that we attain to the highest ethical principles and their understanding only at the conclusion of our striving for wisdom, and also that moral and social communities and endeavors cannot exist without morality. Who has not known someone who was highly developed intellectually, who may have possessed not just a clear intellectual grasp of natural science, but also a good theoretical and practical understanding of many spiritual truths, and yet was not a particularly moral person? Who has not seen clever and highly intelligent people going morally astray? Yet who has not also experienced the other situation, from which we may learn so much? Who has not known someone with a very restricted intellectual horizon and limited knowledge—for example, a nanny, who raised not her own children but those of her employers. She may have nurtured those children from the very first weeks of their physical existence, helped them in their education, and perhaps spent her entire life sacrificing everything for them in an absolutely selfless way, with the utmost devotion imaginable. Yet, if anyone had come to her with moral axioms derived from the very highest founts of wisdom, she probably would not have been much interested. She probably would have found them quite unintelligible and useless. But what she accomplished morally, this is more effective than any acknowledgment of moral axioms. Such cases often cause us to bow down in awe before that which streams from the heart into life and creates so much goodness.

Such facts often answer the riddles of life far more clearly than do theoretical explanations. We see here that a wise Providence did not wait until people had found the moral principles, before providing the world with moral conduct. Thus, if we temporarily disregard immoral acts, whose cause we shall get to know in these lectures, we may say that a divine heritage exists within the human soul, an original goodness that could be called instinctive goodness, which makes it possible for humanity to endure until the moral principles have been discovered.

But perhaps it is quite unnecessary to trouble ourselves so much about discovering moral principles. Might it not be said that it is best if people trust their original moral instincts and do not perplex themselves with theoretical explanations about morality? That this too is not so is just what these lectures are meant to show. They are meant to show that it is necessary for us, at least in the present epoch of humanity, to seek for a theosophical understanding of morality. This understanding must be a task that arises as a fruit of our whole theosophical effort and theosophical science.

Besides much that is quite erroneous in the philosophy of Schopenhauer—a modern philosopher who is certainly also known here in the North—he did say something regarding the principles of morality that is quite correct. He has said, "To preach morality is easy, to establish morality is difficult."[3] This statement is very true, for almost nothing is easier than to pronounce in a manner appealing to the broadest human sentiments, what a person ought to do or leave undone in order to be a good person. Some people might be offended when this is said to be easy, but easy it is, and anyone who knows life, anyone who knows the world, will not doubt that scarcely anything has been more discussed than the correct principles of ethical conduct. And it is particularly true that one meets with almost universal approval when one speaks of these general principles of ethics. It feels so pleasant to the audience, they feel so strongly that they can agree with what the speaker is saying when he discourses on the very broadest principles of human morality.

Moral teaching and moral preaching, however, do not establish morality. Truly not. If morality could be established in this fashion there would certainly be no immorality at this time; humanity would be overflowing with moral actions, for everyone without question has had many opportunities to hear the most beautiful moral principles, especially as people are so fond of preaching them. But knowing what one ought to do, what is morally correct, is of least importance in this realm. What is of most importance, on the other hand, is that there should be impulses living within us, which through their inward strength, their inward power, translate themselves into moral actions. As is well known, moral sermons do not produce this result. Morality can be established only if human beings are guided to sources from which they can receive the impulses that lead to moral conduct.

Just how difficult it is to find these sources is shown by the simple fact that innumerable attempts have been made, for example from the philosophical side, to found a system of ethics, a code of morals. Think how many different answers have been given to the question, "What is the good?" or "What is virtue?" Try collecting all that the philosophers have said, beginning with Plato and Aristotle, passing through the Epicureans, the Stoics, the Neo-Platonists, and down the whole series to the modern philosophers; collect all that has been said about the nature of goodness and virtue—let us just say from Plato to Herbert Spencer—and you will see how many different attempts there have been to penetrate to the sources of moral life and moral impulses.

In these lectures I hope to show that only by delving into the occult secrets of life can one advance, not merely to moral doctrines, but to moral impulses, to the moral sources of life. A single glance suffices, however, to show us that this business of morality is by no means such a simple matter as might be conveniently supposed. Let us for the moment take no notice of what is usually regarded as "moral," and instead consider certain human cultures that may perhaps greatly assist us in developing a moral conception of life.

Among the many things we learn through occultism,[4] not the least is that very diverse conceptions and impulses have held sway among the various peoples in the different parts of the earth. To begin with, then, let us compare two widely separate regions of humanity. Let us go back to the sacred life of ancient India and observe how it unfolded little by little right up into recent times. More so than anywhere else, what was characteristic in ancient times of India and several other Asiatic lands has been preserved right into recent times. The feelings and the thoughts that were found in this region in ancient times have continued into modern times. It is extraordinary how in these cultures an image of former times has been preserved, how when we consider what has been maintained up to our own day, we are at the same time, as it were, looking into the remote past.

Now, we will not progress very far in our understanding of the different peoples on earth if from the beginning we just apply our own moral standards. For this reason, let us for the moment exclude what might be said about the morality of those times and ask only, What has developed from these characteristic features of the ancient Indian culture?

To begin with, we find there that what is most highly revered and respected is what we may call devotion or surrender to the spiritual. And this devotion to the spiritual is the more highly revered the more one is able to sink into oneself, to live within oneself in quietude, and to direct the best in oneself to the heights of the spiritual world, ignoring everything in the physical world. We find that this devotional surrender of the soul to the foundations of existence is the highest duty of those who belonged, or belong, to the highest caste of Indian life, the Brahmans. Everything they do, all their impulses are directed in this way, and nothing impresses the moral sensitivities of the Indian people more than this turning to the divine-spiritual in a mood of deep introspection and self-renunciation, with a devotion that forgets everything physical. The extent to which this attitude permeates the ethical life of this culture may be seen from another fact, namely, that those who belonged to the other castes—especially in ancient times—considered it quite natural for the caste of devotion, the caste of the religious life, to be set apart and venerated. Their whole culture was thus imbued with this impulse to turn to the divine-spiritual, and all of life was placed in service to this. What is involved here cannot be understood with general moral axioms, because in the period when these feelings and impulses were developing in ancient India, it was as yet impossible for them to develop among other peoples. These impulses required the temperament and fundamental character of exactly the Indian people in order to develop the intensity that they did. In the course of civilization they then radiated out from India and spread over the rest of the earth. If we wish to understand what is meant by the divine-spiritual, we must go to this primal source.

Let us now turn our attention away from the Indian culture and direct it toward Europe. Let us consider the peoples of Europe in the period when Christianity was just beginning to enter European culture. You all know that the Christianity spreading into Europe from the East and South was confronted, as it were, by quite definite impulses in the peoples of Europe, by quite definite inner values and forces. One who studies the history of the introduction of Christianity into central Europe, and also here in the North, especially one who studies this with occult means, knows at what cost the balance was struck between this or that Christian impulse and what met it from northern and central Europe.

And now let us ask, as we have already done in the case of the Indian people, What were the prevailing ethical impulses, the moral treasures, the moral heritage, brought to Christianity by those peoples whose descendants constitute the present European population, especially the population of the North, central Europe and England? We need only mention a single one of the principal virtues, and we know at once that we are expressing something that is truly characteristic of these northern and central European peoples. The chief virtue brought by the Europeans to Christianity is expressed in the words "courage" or "fortitude"—the exercise of all the force of one's personality toward actualizing in the physical world one's innermost intentions. The further back we go in time, the more we find that the other virtues are basically derived from this virtue.

If we consider the fundamental nature of true fortitude or courage, we find that it consists of an inner fullness of life that can issue forth. This fullness of life was the most salient characteristic among the ancient inhabitants of Europe. They had within themselves more fullness of life than they could use, and so quite instinctively they followed the impulse to disperse that which they had in superabundance. One could even say that they were wasteful in letting their moral abundance, their fitness, their life impulses pour out into the physical world. Individuals belonging to the ancient European people contained in themselves more than they needed for their own personal use. From this superfluity they could overflow, could be prodigal, could perform their warlike deeds—those deeds of ancient virtue that in modern times are classed as vices. From this superfluity they could also be magnanimous and generous. Acting out of generosity was characteristic of the people of ancient Europe, just as acting out of devotion was characteristic of the people of ancient India.

Theoretical moral axioms would have been of no use to the people of ancient Europe; they would have evinced little understanding for them. Preaching morality to an ancient European would have been like giving someone who does not like math the advice that they ought to precisely record their receipts and expenditures. If such a person does not want to—and if the circumstance is such that they have enough to cover their expenditures—then they do not need to. If their source is inexhaustible, they can dispense with precise bookkeeping. This circumstance is not unimportant; it applies in principle to everything that a person considers of value in life, to everything that engages one's personal activity. With respect to mundane matters, it also applies to the moral feelings of the inhabitants of ancient Europe. Each one had received a divine legacy, as it were, and felt full of it and spent it in service to the family or the tribe, or also in service to larger folk groupings. That was the way they worked and went about life.

We have now characterized two great regions of humanity that are quite different from one another, for the feeling of devotion natural to the Indians did not exist at all among the Europeans. That was why Christianity found it so difficult to bring this feeling of devotion to the Europeans; their predisposition was entirely different.

With these considerations in mind, let us now inquire into their moral effect, without introducing any objections based on moral concepts. It does not take much reflection to see that when these two ways of looking at the world, these two trends of feeling, encountered each other in their purest form, the moral effect was immense. The world has gained infinitely much from what could be achieved only through the existence of a people like the ancient Indians, where all feeling was directed to the devotional surrender to the highest. But the world has also gained infinitely much—and this could be shown in detail—from the courageous deeds of the European peoples of early pre-Christian times. Both of these qualities had to cooperate, and together they have yielded a moral result that has benefited not just a portion of humanity, but all of humanity. In everything that humanity today regards as the highest, we can still see the effect from India as well as the effect from ancient Europe.

Can we say now, without further ado, that this moral result for humanity is "the good"? Yes we can, without a doubt. Certainly within both of these cultures it must be the good, and something must exist that we can designate as the good. Yet, if we wish to say what the good is, we are again confronted by a riddle. What is the good which has worked in the one case as well as in the other?

I do not wish to give you a moral sermon, for I do not consider this to be my task. Rather, I regard it as my task to present facts to you which can lead to a theosophical conception of morality. For this reason I have initially placed before you two sets of known historical facts, and I ask you to note only that the fact of devotion and the fact of courage produce definite moral effects in the cultural evolution of humanity.

Let us now turn our attention to a different time period. If you look at the moral impulses present in modern life, you will naturally say that today—at least in Europe—we cannot conform to the purest ideal of ancient India, because European culture cannot be maintained with Indian devotionalism. But it would be just as impossible for us to gain modern European culture with the ancient European peoples' praiseworthy virtue of fortitude. We see at once that there is still something different about the ethics of the ancient Europeans. We must search still further, therefore, to be able to answer the question: What is goodness? What is virtue?

I have often pointed out that we have to distinguish between the period we call the Greco-Latin or fourth post-Atlantean cultural epoch and the fifth post-Atlantean epoch, which we live in at the present time.[5] And what I have now to say regarding the nature of morality is really intended to characterize the origin of the fifth post-Atlantean epoch. Let us begin with something which you may consider open to doubt, since it is taken from poetry and legend, but which is still characteristic of the way that fresh moral impulses became active and gradually flowed into humanity as the fifth post-Atlantean epoch began to unfold.

There was a poet who lived around the end of the twelfth century and beginning of the thirteenth. He died in the year 1213 and he was known as Hartmann von Aue.[6] This poet's most important poem—*Der arme Heinrich* ["Poor Henry"]—was written completely out of the mode of thinking and feeling prevalent in his day. It expresses especially well how certain moral impulses were regarded in particular circles and regions at that time. This is the gist of it: Originally Poor Henry was not poor, but was a rich and well-appointed knight. He took no account, however, that the sense-perceptible things of the physical world are but transient and fleeting; he lived only for the world and rapidly engendered unfavorable karma. He was thus stricken with a form of leprosy, and although he visited all the most celebrated physicians, none of them could help him. So, giving up his life for lost, he sold all his possessions and, because his disease did not allow him to live in society, retired to a solitary farm where he was loyally nursed by an old devoted servant and the servant's daughter. One day the daughter and the whole household learn that there is only one thing that can help the knight who has this destiny. No physician, no medicines can help him; only if a pure virgin sacrifices her life for him out of love can his health be restored. In spite of all the exhortations of her parents and of the knight Henry himself, something comes over the daughter which makes her believe that she is the one who should sacrifice herself. So she goes with the knight to Salerno, the most celebrated medical school of the time, and does not shrink from what the physicians require of her. She is ready to sacrifice her life. But the knight does not allow this to happen; he prevents it and returns home with her. The poem then tells us that when the knight returned home, he actually began to recover, and that he lived for a long time and spent a happy old age with the one who had been determined to save him.

Well, you may say, this is a poem after all, and we need not take literally the things spoken of here. But the matter begins to look different when we compare what Hartmann von Aue wrote in *Der arme Heinrich* with something that we know actually happened, when we compare what Hartmann von Aue expressed with the life and deeds of an actual person living in Italy at that time. I mean Francis of Assisi, who was born in 1182.[7]

Now, in order to describe the moral nature that was concentrated, as it were, in the single personality of Francis of Assisi, let us consider the matter as it appears to the occult investigator, even if this causes us to appear foolish and superstitious. Let us take seriously what I am going to describe, for in that time of transition these things were taken very seriously.

We know that Francis of Assisi was the son of the Italian merchant Bernardone and his wife. We know that the father traveled a great deal in France, where he carried on his business, and that he was a man who placed great value on outer appearances. The mother of Francis of Assisi had the virtue of piety and other fine qualities of the heart, and lived devoutly according to her religious feelings. Now, the things that are recounted in the form of legends about the birth and the life of Francis of Assisi are entirely in agreement with occult facts. Although history frequently veils occult facts in pictures and legends, these legends do correspond with the occult facts. Thus it is quite true that before the birth of Francis of Assisi, a great number of people knew through visionary revelations that an important person was about to be born. History records that one of the many people who dreamt— that is, who saw in prophetic vision—that an important person was about to be born, was Saint Hildegard.[8] (I must emphasize once more the truth of these facts, which can be corroborated by investigations in the Akasha Chronicle.)[9] She dreamt that a woman appeared to her, whose face was scratched and covered with blood, and who said, "The birds have their nests here upon the earth, the foxes too have their holes, but at present I have nothing, not even a staff to lean on." When Hildegard awakened, she knew that this personality represented the true face of Christianity.[10] And many other persons dreamt in a similar manner. They realized that the external institution of the Church was unfit to be a receptacle, a sheath for the real Christianity.

One day, while Francis' father was on business in France— this again is a fact—a pilgrim came to Donna Pica's house, to the mother of Francis of Assisi, and said to her, "The child you are expecting must not be born in this house, where there is abundance; you must give birth to him in the stable, for he must lie upon straw and so follow after his Master!" This was actually said to the mother of Francis of Assisi; and it is not legend but truth that because the father was in France on business, the mother was able to carry this out, so that Francis of Assisi was actually born in a stable upon straw. And another thing is also true: Some time after the child was born, a strange man came into the little town, a man never been seen in that neighborhood before and never seen there again. He went back and forth through the streets saying, "An important person has been born in this town." And those persons who could still lead a healthy visionary life also heard bells ringing at the time of the birth of Francis of Assisi.

A whole series of phenomena could be mentioned, but we will content ourselves with these, which have been mentioned only to show how everything from the spiritual world was meaningfully concentrated relative to the advent of a single person of that time. And this all becomes especially interesting when one further thing is considered. The mother had the peculiar impression that the child ought to be called "John," and he was therefore given this name. When the father returned, however, he gave his son the name Francis, because he wished to commemorate his successful business journey to France. But originally the child was named John.[11]

We need to dwell now on just a few details from the life of this remarkable man, especially from his youth. What sort of a person was Francis of Assisi as a youth? He was someone who conducted himself like a descendant of the ancient Germanic warriors, which need not appear remarkable to us if we consider how the peoples had intermixed after the immigrations from the North. He was brave and warlike, and filled with the ideal of winning honor and fame with the weapons of war; that was what existed like a heritage, like a racial characteristic, in the personality of Francis of Assisi. He also expressed in a more external way, one might say, the same qualities that existed as a more inward quality of soul in the ancient Germans, for in his youth, Francis of Assisi was what one calls a spendthrift. At every opportunity he squandered the possessions of his father, who was at the time a rich man. Francis lavished the fruits of his father's labor on all his comrades and playfellows. Little wonder then that his comrades chose him to lead their youthful warlike expeditions, and that as he grew up he was looked upon as a truly warlike boy, for such was his reputation throughout the whole town. He took part in the various feuds between the youths of the towns of Assisi and Perugia, and it thus came about on one occasion that he and his comrades were taken prisoner. He then not only bore his own captivity in knightly fashion, but also inspired the others to do the same, until after a year they were able to return home.

Later on, when a military expedition against Naples was being prepared, which those in the knighthood were required to join, it happened that this young man had a dream-vision. He saw a great palace, wherein were stored all kinds of weapons and shields. Prior to this he had seen in his father's house and place of business only numerous kinds of cloth, and thus he said to himself, "This is a summons for me to become a soldier!" So he resolved to join the expedition against Naples; but as he was preparing to do this, and even more so after he had joined the expedition, he received spiritual impressions, spiritual messages. He heard something like a voice, which said, "Go no further, you have wrongly interpreted this important dream. Go back to Assisi and you will learn how to interpret it correctly." He obeyed these words, went back to Assisi, and there had something like an inner dialogue with a being who spoke to him spiritually and said, "Do not seek your knighthood in external service. You are destined to transform all the forces at your disposal into powers of soul, into weapons to be used by your soul. The weapons you saw in the palace signify the spiritual weapons of mercy, compassion and love. The shields signify the good sense you must exercise in order to withstand the trials of a life dedicated to mercy, compassion and love." Thereafter he had a short but dangerous illness. He recovered from this and then passed through something like a retrospect of his whole life, which lasted for several days. The young knight who in his boldest dreams had only longed to become a hero in battle, was reforged, as it were, into a man who was now utterly dedicated to spreading the moral impulses of mercy, compassion and love. All the forces that he had wanted to use in service to the physical world were transformed into inner moral impulses.

We see here how a moral impulse is aroused in a single person. It is not unimportant that in this case we are studying a great moral impulse, for although an individual person cannot always attain to the greatest ethical heights, it is only where impulses are expressed most radically and with the greatest forcefulness that an individual can learn from them. It is precisely by turning our attention to what is most radical—and by considering lesser things in the light of this radical greatness—that we come to a correct conception about the moral impulses of life.

What happened next to Francis of Assisi? It is not necessary to describe the disputes he had with his father as he now became prodigal in an entirely different manner. The father could understand his son's earlier extravagance, which was also advantageous in that it brought his house fame and esteem, but he could not understand now how his son could cast off his best clothes and even his necessities and give them to those in need. And the father could not understand his son's frame of mind when the son said, "It is remarkable how little respect is given to those who have done so much for the Christian impulse in the West," and then proceeded to make a pilgrimage to Rome to lay a large sum of money at the graves of the Apostles Peter and Paul. These things his father did not understand. I need not describe the disputes that took place; I need only point out that for Francis of Assisi all the impulses of morality became concentrated through these disputes. These concentrated impulses transformed the fortitude in his soul and then developed in such a way that they were greatly strengthened by his meditations and appeared before him as the Cross with the Crucified One. In this condition he felt an inner, personal relationship to the Cross and to the Christ; and from this relationship there then came to him the forces that could augment so immeasurably the moral impulses that now filled him.

He found a remarkable use for what now unfolded within him. In those days the horrors of leprosy had spread over many parts of Europe, and the Church had come up with a strange cure for the lepers who were then so numerous. The priests would call the lepers and say to them, "You are stricken with this disease in this life, but inasmuch as you are lost to this life, you have been won for God, you are consecrated to God." Then, however, the lepers were sent away from other people, to desolate places where they had to spend the rest of their lives alone.

I do not want to blame the priests for this kind of cure; they knew no better. But Francis of Assisi knew a better one. I am mentioning all this because it will lead us to the sources of morality from actual experience; you will see in the next lectures why we are dealing with these things. Francis of Assisi was impelled by this state of affairs to go everywhere and search out all the lepers, and to be unafraid of associating with them. And in fact, that which none of the remedies of the time could cure, and which therefore made it necessary to exclude these people from human society, this sickness was healed by Francis of Assisi in numberless cases. He went to the lepers with the power that existed in his moral impulses, and these allowed him no fear, but rather gave him the courage not only to carefully cleanse their sores, but also to live with them, to nurse them fully, even to kiss them, to transfuse them with his love.[12]

The healing of Poor Henry by the daughter of his faithful servant is not just a poetic story; it expresses what actually occurred in a great number of cases at that time through the historically well-known personality of Francis of Assisi. Note carefully what took place there. In someone like Francis of Assisi there existed a tremendous fund of psychic energy, something which had existed as courage and fortitude in the ancient peoples of Europe, but which in him had been transformed and thereafter acted on the level of soul and spirit. Just as what worked as generosity and fortitude in ancient times had led to an expenditure of personal force, and had manifested in Francis of Assisi in his younger days as compulsive extravagance, so this now led him to become prodigal of moral force. He was full to overflowing with moral force, and this passed over to those to whom he turned his love.

You must realize that this moral force is a reality, just as much a reality as the air we breathe, without which we could not live. It is a reality which flooded the whole being of Francis of Assisi and from there streamed into every heart he turned to, for Francis of Assisi was prodigal of a wealth of forces. This reality is something that has streamed into and mingled with the whole mature life of Europe; it is something that has been transformed into a force of soul and worked in this way into the outer world.

Try to reflect on these facts, which at first may apparently have nothing to do with the actual question of morality. Try to grasp what is contained in Indian devotion and Nordic courage. Think about the healing effect of such moral forces as were exercised by Francis of Assisi. Then tomorrow we shall be able to speak about what real moral impulses are, and we shall see that it is not merely words but realities that are at work in the soul and that establish morality.

LECTURE TWO

May 29, 1912

I remarked yesterday that what is to be said here about theosophical moral principles and impulses should be built on facts, and for this reason I tried to bring forward a few historical facts that clearly demonstrated moral impulses. With the example of Francis of Assisi, it is clear that enormous moral impulses must have been at work in order for him to have been able to do the deeds that he did. For what kind of deeds were they? They were deeds that demonstrated morality in the very highest sense of the word. Francis of Assisi was surrounded by people afflicted with very serious diseases, which the rest of the world at that time did not know how to cure. The moral forces that streamed out from him did not merely give comfort to their souls—though certainly in many cases that was all that could be achieved—but also had healing, health-giving effects for those with sufficient faith and trust.

Now, to understand more deeply the origin of the moral impulses of such an outstanding personality as Francis of Assisi, we must ask ourselves how it came about that he could develop such forces. What took place with him? To understand what was active in the soul of this extraordinary human being, we must cast our gaze somewhat further afield.

Recall that in the ancient civilization of India the people were divided into four castes, and that the highest of these was the caste of the Brahmans, the cultivators of wisdom. The separation of the castes in ancient India was so strict that the sacred books, for example, could be read solely by the Brahmans and not by members of the other castes. The members of the second caste, the Warriors, could not read, but only hear, the sacred doctrine contained in the Vedas, or in the epitome of the Vedas, the Vedanta.[13] The Brahmans alone were allowed to explain or interpret any passage from the Vedas; anyone else was strictly forbidden to have an opinion about what was contained in the sacred books. The second caste consisted of those in the military profession and those involved in governing the country. Then there was a third caste of those responsible for trade and commerce, and also a fourth, a laboring caste. Last of all, however, were the Pariahs, who were an utterly despised part of the population. They were so despised that a Brahman who so much as stepped on a Pariah's shadow felt contaminated and even had to perform certain purification rites. Thus we see how the whole society was divided into four recognized castes, and one that was absolutely unrecognized. Is it really possible that such severe rules were observed in ancient India? They were indeed observed, and strictly so. Even at the time of the Greco-Latin period in Europe, no member of the Warrior caste in India would ever have ventured to have a personal opinion about anything in the sacred Vedas.

Now, how and why did such a division of human beings arise? It is strange that we find this caste system precisely among the most advanced people of antiquity, among those who had migrated from ancient Atlantis over to India already in comparatively early times, and who had preserved the greatest store of wisdom from ancient Atlantis.[14] This seems very strange. How can we comprehend something like this? It seems as if it would contradict all the wisdom and goodness in the guidance of the world, for the highest treasure to be preserved by one group alone, while other human beings are predestined by the mere fact of their birth to occupy subordinate positions.

This can be understood only if we cast a glance into the secrets of existence. Evolution is possible only by means of differentiation and separation; if everyone had wished to arrive at the degree of wisdom attained in the Brahman caste, no one would have been able to reach it. Divine world guidance is not contradicted by the fact that highest wisdom is not always attained in the same way. To demand this would make no more sense than to demand that an omniscient and omnipotent God should make a triangle with four corners. No god can make a triangle other than with three corners. What is inwardly ordered and determined must also be adhered to by the divine powers; the laws of evolution are as strict as the laws of space. Just as a triangle can have but three corners, so too must evolution occur via differentiation. In order for special qualities to develop in human evolution, certain groups of human beings must be separated off for a time. This is not just a law of human evolution, it is a law of all evolution.

Consider the form of the human body. You will certainly admit that the most perfected and valuable parts of the human form are the bones of the head. But how was it possible for these particular bones to become skull bones and envelop the noble organ of the brain? Every human bone is potentially a skull bone, but in order for some to actually develop to this height—to become sheaths for the front or the back of the head—the hip bones or the wrist bones had to remain at a lower stage of development.

It is this way everywhere; progress is possible only if some remain behind while others advance ahead and even overshoot a certain point of development. The Brahmans advanced beyond a certain average point of development, while the lowest castes remained behind this point.

As the Atlantean catastrophe was beginning, groups of people in Atlantis—the ancient continent located where the Atlantic Ocean is today—gradually migrated eastward and populated the lands now known as Europe, Asia and Africa. (We will not consider today the groups who migrated westward, whose descendants were later discovered in America.) The body of people who migrated eastward consisted not just of the four castes who settled in India; there were actually seven castes, and the four who settled in India were actually the four higher castes. Apart from the fifth caste—the Pariahs—who formed the interstitial substance, as it were, of the population in India, there were also other castes who did not migrate to India but who remained in various places in Europe, Asia Minor and also in Africa. Thus, in fact, only the most select castes migrated to India, and those who remained behind in Europe had quite different qualities from those who went on to India.

Indeed, one only understands what later took place in Europe when one knows that the more advanced portions of humanity in those days went on to Asia, and that the main body of the population left behind in Europe provided the opportunity for quite particular incarnations. If we wish to understand the nature of the particular souls who incarnated into the bulk of the ancient European population, we must call to mind a certain event that took place in Atlantean times. At a certain time during the Atlantean age it happened that great secrets of existence were betrayed, secrets that are much more profound than any to which post-Atlantean civilization has attained. These secrets needed to be limited to small circles but were instead betrayed to large parts of the Atlantean population, who thereby acquired occult knowledge for which they were not yet ripe. As a consequence, their souls were strongly driven into a condition of moral decline, and only those who later migrated to Asia remained on the path of goodness.[15]

However, you must not imagine that the whole European population consisted only of people in whose souls were individuals who had suffered a moral downfall due to the temptations they had been exposed to during Atlantean times. Scattered throughout this European population were others who had not migrated to Asia but who had remained behind to act as leaders. Thus, over large areas of Europe, Asia Minor and Africa, we have human beings who belonged, as it were, to castes or races that allowed fallen souls to live in their bodies.[16] But besides these, there were also better, more highly developed souls who had not migrated to India and who could take over the leadership.

The best regions for those souls who took on the leadership at that time—the period when the Indian and Persian civilizations developed—were the more northerly parts of Europe, the regions where the oldest European Mystery Centers flourished.[17] A kind of protective arrangement was instituted to guard against what had happened earlier in ancient Atlantis. In Atlantis, the souls we have described were tempted through being given occult knowledge and wisdom for which they were unprepared. For this reason, in the European Mystery Centers, the store of wisdom had to be protected and guarded all the more. Those who were the actual teachers of wisdom in Europe in the post-Atlantean period withdrew themselves completely and preserved what they had received as a strict secret. One can thus say that also in

Europe there were persons comparable to the Brahmans of Asia; but these European Brahmans were not outwardly known as such by anyone. They kept the sacred secrets absolutely secluded in the Mystery Centers, so there would be no repetition of what had already happened once in ancient Atlantis. Only through the most careful protection and guardianship of the store of wisdom was it possible for the fallen souls to be able to uplift themselves in certain respects. For indeed, the differentiation of humanity does not occur in such a manner that one portion is predestined for a lower rank than another. Rather, what is lower at one time should rise upward at a later time; but for this the requisite conditions must be created. In this way it came about that in Europe there were souls who had fallen into temptation, who had lost their moral cohesiveness, while among them a wisdom was working from deeply hidden sources.[18]

Furthermore, in Europe there were also members of the other castes who had gone to India. In Europe it was primarily members of the second Indian caste—the Warrior caste—who took on positions of power. Whereas the wise teachers—those who corresponded to the Indian Brahmans—withdrew entirely and gave their counsel from hidden stations, the Warriors came out among the people to improve and advance them in accordance with the counsels of those European teachers and priests. This second caste wielded the greatest power in ancient Europe, but their life was guided by the wise priests who remained hidden. Thus it came about that the prominent personalities of Europe were those who distinguished themselves with the qualities we spoke of yesterday—with courage and fortitude. Whereas in India wisdom was exalted because the Brahmans interpreted the sacred writings, in Europe fortitude was held in highest esteem, and the prominent personalities knew only where they must go to get the divine secrets, which they then had to infuse into their courage and fortitude.

Looking on the course of European culture over thousands and thousands of years, we see how the souls were gradually improved and elevated. However, because most of the people in Europe were descendants of the population that had fallen into temptation, no proper appreciation for the caste system of India could develop. The people there became all mixed together. A differentiation, a division into castes as in India, did not occur. The only division was between those who were the leaders—an upper class, which later developed in the most varied directions—and those who were led. The latter consisted mainly of souls who had to struggle to uplift themselves.

If we seek those souls who gradually struggled upward out of this lower class, who raised themselves from their fallen state, we find them chiefly in the European population of which today's history books tell but little. Century after century this population developed itself in order to rise to a higher stage, to recover, as it were, from the heavy setback it had received in the Atlantean period. Thus, whereas Asian culture progressed continuously, in Europe the process was more of a recovery, a reversal of the moral downfall into a gradual moral improvement. Things went on in this way for a long time, and improvement came about only because the human soul contains an extraordinary instinct to imitate. Those who were courageously active among the folk were regarded as the models—as the "first" [German: *Fürsten*]—and were imitated by the others. Thus, through these persons who mingled with the folk as leaders, the morality of all of Europe was raised.

With this, however, something else became necessary in European evolution, and to understand this, we must make a clear distinction between the evolution of a single soul and that of a whole race. The two must not be confused. A human soul can develop in such a way that in one incarnation it embodies itself in a particular race, and, if it thereby acquires certain qualities, then in a later incarnation it can re-embody itself in an entirely different race. Thus, within the European population of today, we can certainly discover souls whose previous incarnations were in India, Japan or China. Souls do not by any means stay with the same race. Soul evolution is something quite different from racial evolution, which proceeds at its own pace.

In ancient Europe, the situation was such that the souls who had fallen into temptation were incarnated in the European races because they could not enter into the Asiatic races; and these souls were obliged at that time to incarnate repeatedly in the European races. As they improved themselves, however, they gradually passed over into higher races. Souls previously incarnated in quite subordinate races, raised themselves to a higher level and could then incarnate in the bodily descendants of the leaders in Europe. As more and more souls developed themselves, the bodily descendants of the leaders became more and more numerous, and the bodily form in which the bulk of the ancient European population had originally incarnated, entirely died out as a physical race. The souls, as it were, abandoned the bodies that were formed in a particular way, and these then died out. This was the reason that the lower races had fewer and fewer descendants, while the higher races had more and more. Gradually the lowest levels of the European population completely died out.[19]

This is a very specific process, which we must understand. The souls develop further, but the bodies die out. That is why we must distinguish so carefully between soul evolution and racial evolution. The souls reappear in bodies belonging to higher races, while the bodies of the lower races die out. Such a process, however, does not occur without having effects of its own. When something like this occurs over large regions, when something disappears, as it were, it does not disappear into nothing, but rather disperses and is then present in a different form. You will understand what I mean if you consider that with the dying out of the worst parts of the ancient population of which I have been speaking, the whole region gradually became filled with demonic beings that represented the products of decay of what had died out. The whole of Europe and also Asia Minor were thus filled with the spiritual products of decay from the dying out of the worst parts of the population. These demons of decay, which were contained in the spiritual atmosphere, as it were, endured for a long time and later exerted an influence in such a way that they permeated people's feelings. Their influence can best be seen at the time of the Great Migrations, when large masses of people, including Attila and his hordes,[20] came over from Asia and caused great terror among the people in Europe. This terror made the population susceptible to the influences of the demonic beings that still persisted from earlier times. As a consequence of the terror produced by the hordes coming over from Asia, there gradually developed what manifested during the Middle Ages as the epidemic of leprosy. This disease was nothing other than the consequence of the conditions of fear and terror that the people experienced at that time. But these conditions could have had this effect only with people who had been exposed to the demonic forces from the past.

I have now described to you how it was possible for people to succumb to a disease that was later practically eradicated in Europe, and why it was so widespread during the period I characterized in the first lecture. Thus we see how certain races have died out, as they needed to because they did not develop upwards, but also how we still have their aftereffects in the form of human diseases. In the disease of leprosy we see the consequence of soul-spiritual causes.

This whole situation had now to be counteracted. Further development in Europe could come about only if what I have described to you were entirely removed. An example of how it was removed was given in yesterday's lecture, where I showed that although the aftereffects of immorality were present as the demons of disease, strong moral impulses were present too, as in Francis of Assisi. Because Francis of Assisi had such strong moral impulses, he also gathered around him others who worked in the same way, albeit to a lesser degree. At that time there were actually quite a few who worked in this way; it only did not last for long.

How did such a soul-power enter into Francis of Assisi? Since we are not gathered here to study external science, but to understand human morality from its occult foundations, we must now examine a few occult truths. Let us then inquire: Whence really came such a soul as that of Francis of Assisi? Such a soul can be understood only if we take the trouble to investigate what was hidden in its depths. Here I must remind you that the old division into castes in India really received its first blow, its first shock, through Buddhism, for among the many other things that Buddhism introduced into Asiatic life was the idea that the caste system was not justified. As far as it was possible in Asia, Buddhism recognized each human being as a candidate for the highest. You know too that all this was only possible through the outstandingly great and mighty personality of the Buddha.[21] You know that the Buddha became a Buddha in the incarnation we are usually told of, and that in the earlier part of this life he was a Bodhisattva, which represents the rank just below Buddhahood. In his twenty-ninth year of life this son of King Suddhodana had deeply experienced the great truths about life and sorrow, and through this he had acquired the greatness to introduce into Asia the teaching known as Buddhism.

We must keep something else in mind, however, which was also connected with this advancement from Bodhisattva to Buddha. When this individuality who had passed through many incarnations as a Bodhisattva advanced to the rank of a Buddha, that incarnation became his last incarnation on earth in a physical body. One who is raised from Bodhisattva to Buddha has thereby entered a final incarnation; from then onward such an individuality works only spiritually. Thus, since the fifth century B.C., the individuality of the Buddha has worked exclusively from spiritual heights.

Buddhism, however, has continued. It was able to influence in a certain way not just Asiatic life, but also the cultural life of the whole of the then known world. You know how Buddhism has spread in Asia and how many followers it has there, but in a more hidden and veiled form it has also spread within the cultural life of Europe. In particular, the portion of the Buddha's great teaching that related to human equality was especially suited to the population of Europe, because that population was not based on a caste system, but was instead directed toward the idea of equality. Some centuries into the Christian era, a kind of occult school was founded on the shores of the Black Sea.[22] This school was led by people who had as their highest ideal the part of the Buddha's teaching that we have just characterized. But the teachers in this school could illuminate the Buddha's teaching with a new light, as it were, because they had also absorbed the Christian impulse. If I were to describe this school on the Black Sea as it is viewed by the occultist—and you will understand me best if I do so—I must do this in the following manner.

Pupils were gathered there who initially had teachers on the outer, physical plane. These pupils were instructed in doctrines and principles which had originated in Buddhism, but which were permeated by the impulses that came into the world through Christianity. Then, when the pupils were sufficiently prepared, the deeper forces of wisdom within them were brought forth, so that they acquired a clairvoyant vision of the spiritual world. One of the first things attained by the pupils of this occult school, after the teachers on the physical plane had accustomed them to it, was the ability to recognize those who no longer descended to the physical plane. In this way they came to know the Buddha, for example. Indeed, these occult pupils learned to know the Buddha "face to face," if one may speak in this way of his spiritual being. Thus the Buddha continued to work spiritually in the occult pupils; in this manner he brought his power down to the physical plane, since he himself no longer descended to physical incarnation on the physical plane.

The pupils in this occult school were divided into two groups, according to their degree of maturity. This refers to those pupils who had already gone through the preparatory stage, so that most of them could clairvoyantly experience a being who strove with all its might to bring its impulses through to the physical world, even though it did not itself descend to the physical plane. They thus experienced all the secrets of the Buddha and all that he wished to accomplish. Most of these pupils remained clairvoyants as such, but there were some who not only had knowledge and psychic clairvoyance, but who also developed a spiritual element, which cannot be separated from a certain humility, a certain highly evolved capacity for devotion. These were able then, precisely in this occult school, to receive the Christ Impulse to a tremendous degree. They could also become clairvoyant in such a way that they became the specially chosen successors of Paul and received the Christ Impulse directly into their life.[23] Thus two groups went out from this school, one which had the impulse to spread the teachings of the Buddha—though they did not use his name—and a second one which also received the Christ Impulse.

Now the difference between these two groups did not appear so strongly in that particular incarnation, but only in the next. The pupils who had come as far as the Buddha Impulse, but who had not received the Christ Impulse, became the teachers of human equality and brotherhood. On the other hand, the pupils who had received the Christ Impulse, were such that in their next physical incarnation the Christ Impulse worked on further, so that they not only could teach—though they did not regard this as their chief task—but could work more especially through their moral power. One such pupil of the occult school on the Black Sea was born in his next incarnation as Francis of Assisi. It is not surprising, then, that there lived in him the wisdom he had received about brotherhood and human equality, about the need to love all human beings equally, and that his soul was permeated and strengthened by the Christ Impulse.

How did this Christ Impulse work on further in Francis of Assisi? It acted in such a way that when he was placed in a population in which the old demons of disease were especially active, the Christ Impulse approached the disease-demons through him and absorbed their evil substance into itself, thereby removing it from the people. Earlier the Christ Impulse had embodied itself in this substance in such a way that it appeared to Francis of Assisi as a vision—as the vision in which he saw the palace and was called to take up the burden of poverty. This was the point at which the Christ Impulse again became alive in him, and it then streamed out from him and laid hold of the disease-demons. His moral forces became so strong thereby that they could remove the harmful spiritual substances that accompanied the disease we have mentioned. Only in this manner was it possible to bring to higher development what I have described as the aftereffect of the old Atlantean element, to sweep the evil substances away from the earth and purify the European world.

Look at the life of Francis of Assisi and notice how remarkably it unfolded. He is born in the year 1182. We know that the first years of life of a human being are largely devoted to the development of the physical body. The physical body manifests chiefly what comes via external heredity. Hence there appears in him what he inherited from the European population. His own special qualities gradually appear as he develops his etheric body between the ages of seven and fourteen.[24] From the etheric body especially the quality appears that had worked directly in him as the Christ Impulse in the Mystery Center by the Black Sea.[25] Then, as his astral body comes to manifestation after age fourteen, the Christ-force becomes particularly enlivened in him as his astral body takes up what has remained united with the atmosphere of the earth since the Mystery of Golgotha.[26] For Francis of Assisi was a personality also permeated by the outer Christ-force, because in his previous incarnation he had sought the Christ-force where it was to be found—in that special center of initiation.

Here we see how the process of differentiation works in humanity. Differentiation must come about, but what is pushed downward through earlier events is later uplifted through very special occurrences in the course of human evolution. There was another occasion when a particularly important uplifting took place in the evolution of humanity, one which exoterically will always remain incomprehensible. People have given up trying to understand it, but esoterically it can be fully explained. Those who had raised themselves up most quickly from the lowest strata of the Western population, who had gradually overcome their passage through the lowest strata but who had not developed their intellect very much and had remained relatively simple people—the most select of these, as it were, who needed only to be uplifted at the appointed time by a mighty impulse that reflected itself in them—they are known to us as the Twelve Apostles of Jesus. They were the extract of the lower castes who were diverted and did not go on to India. The substance for the disciples of Christ Jesus had to be taken from these castes. I am not saying anything here about the previous or subsequent incarnations of the apostle individualities, only about the physical ancestry of the bodies into which the apostle personalities were incarnated. One must always distinguish between the incarnation lineage and the lineage of physical heredity.[27]

We have now found the source of the moral power of that unique personality, Francis of Assisi. Do not say that it would be too much to expect people to adopt such extraordinary ideals as existed with Francis of Assisi. What I have said was certainly not said in order to recommend that anyone become a Francis of Assisi. Not at all. I just wished to point out, by means of a particularly striking example, how moral power can enter into a human being, whence it can originate, and how it must be understood as something very special that was originally present in the human being. However, from the whole spirit of what I have said up to now you may gather what we have also often emphasized regarding other forces in human evolution: namely, that humanity has gone through a descent and is now undertaking an ascent.

If we journey back in human evolution, we pass through the post-Atlantean age to the Atlantean catastrophe, then to the Atlantean age, and then further back to the Lemurian age. We thus arrive at the starting-point of earthly humanity, at a time when humanity was much closer to the divine, not only with regard to the qualities of spirit but also with regard to morality. At the beginning of earth evolution we do not find immorality but rather morality. Morality is an original, divine gift, part of the original content of human nature, just as spiritual power was part of human nature when humanity had not descended so far. In truth, a large part of immorality entered human evolution in just the way I have described, by means of the betrayal of higher Mysteries during the ancient Atlantean age.

Thus we cannot speak about morality as if it were something that humanity first had to develop; morality is something that lies at the foundation of the human soul, and has been hidden and suppressed only by later civilization. When we look at the matter in the right light, we cannot even say that immorality came into the world through folly. Rather, it came into the world because the Mysteries were betrayed to human beings who were still immature. In this way, people were tempted and then succumbed and degenerated. In order for them to rise again—you can gather this from today's presentation—something was needed that would sweep away everything that had set itself against the moral impulse in the human soul.

Let me put this another way. Let us suppose we have before us a criminal, someone we call immoral; on no account may we say that there are no moral impulses in this immoral person. They are there and we shall find them if we go to the foundation of his or her soul. There is no human soul—with the exception of black magicians, who are not our concern here—in which there is not a foundation of goodness. If a person is bad, it is because what has arisen in the course of time as spiritual error has overlain the goodness. Human nature is not bad; originally it was good.

Concrete observation of human nature shows us that in its deepest nature it is good, and that it was the subsequent spiritual errors that diverted people from the path of goodness. Therefore, in the course of time, people must correct these moral errors. The errors themselves and also their consequences must be rectified. However, where the consequences of immorality are so severe that demons of disease exist, then super-moral forces like those of Francis of Assisi must also be active.

The betterment of human beings always involves eliminating their spiritual errors; but what is needed for this? Take everything I have now told you and condense it into one basic mood or feeling. Let the facts speak to you, let them speak to your feelings and try to gather them together into one fundamental feeling. You will then say to yourself: "What attitude toward other people does one need to have? One needs to believe in their original goodness, in the original goodness of each human being!" This is the first thing we must say if we attempt to speak at all about morality—that there is an unfathomable goodness at the foundation of human nature. That is what Francis of Assisi said to himself. And when he was approached by some of those afflicted with the dreadful disease of leprosy, then as a good Christian of that time he said somewhat the following to himself: "Such a disease is in some respect the result of sin, but because sin is spiritual error, because the disease is the consequence of spiritual error, it must therefore be canceled and removed by a strong opposite spiritual power." Thus Francis of Assisi saw how in some respects the penalty of sin revealed itself outwardly on the sinner. But he also saw the goodness of human nature, the divine-spiritual powers at the foundation of every human soul. This tremendous faith in the goodness of every human soul, even in those being punished, was what especially distinguished Francis of Assisi. Through this faith it was possible for the power that is opposed to sin to appear in his soul, the power of love that strengthens, comforts, and indeed even heals. And no one who has fully developed the impulse of faith in the original goodness of human nature, can do otherwise than love this human nature as such.

It is these two fundamental impulses, to begin with, that can establish a truly moral life: First, the faith in the divine at the foundation of every human soul, and second, the boundless love of humanity that springs from this faith. For only this boundless love could lead Francis of Assisi to the ailing, the crippled, and those stricken with the plague. And then there is a third thing that is necessarily founded on the first two. A person who has a foundation of faith in the goodness of the human soul and in the love of human nature can do no other than say: What arises from the combination of the original goodness of the human soul and active love justifies a perspective on the future wherein every soul, no matter how far it has fallen from spiritual heights, may be led back again to these heights. This is the third impulse, the hope that every human soul can find its way back to the divine-spiritual world.

We can say that Francis of Assisi heard these three impulses expressed countless times, that they were repeatedly brought to his attention during his initiation into the Colchian Mysteries by the Black Sea. We can also say, however, that in his life as Francis of Assisi, he preached very little of faith and love; instead, he was himself an embodiment of this faith and this love. In him these appeared as a living symbol before the world. Foremost, of course, was that which really works. For faith does not work and neither does hope; these one must indeed have, but only love works. Love stands in the center, and love is what carried the actual moral development of humanity toward the divine during this incarnation of Francis of Assisi.[28]

This love, which we know was a result of his initiation in the Mysteries at Colchis, how have we seen it unfold in him? We saw that the warlike virtues of the ancient European spirit appeared in Francis of Assisi, that he was a warlike boy. But in his individuality, permeated as it was by the Christ Impulse, courage and fortitude were transformed into active, effective love. We see the ancient courage and fortitude resurrected, as it were, in the love that we encounter in Francis of Assisi. Courage transformed into spirituality, spiritualized ancient fortitude—these are love!

It is interesting to notice how much of what has just been said also corresponds to the outer historical development of humanity. If we go back a few centuries into pre-Christian times, into the fourth post-Atlantean epoch, we find the Greek philosopher Plato who wrote, among other things, about morals, about human virtues.[29] He described them in such a way that we can recognize that he held back the highest secrets, but that what he could say, he put into the mouth of Socrates. Writing at a time in European history in which the Christ Impulse was not yet active, Plato describes what he views as the highest virtues, the virtues the Greeks felt a moral person should have above all else. To begin with, Plato describes three primary virtues (we shall also get to know a fourth one). The first virtue is that of wisdom. Plato regards wisdom as such as a virtue. We have seen wisdom justified as the basis of moral life from the most varied directions. In India the wisdom of the Brahmans was the basis of life; in Europe the wisdom was more hidden, but it lived in the Northern Mysteries where the European Brahmans were engaged in remedying what had been damaged through the betrayal in ancient Atlantis. As we shall see tomorrow, wisdom does indeed stand behind all morality. Then, in keeping with the Mysteries from which he drew,[30] Plato also describes courage as a virtue, which we find mainly in the

European population. As a third virtue he designates "temper-ance" or "self-discipline" [*Besonnenheit, Mässigkeit*]—in other words, the opposite of a passionate cultivation of the lower human drives. Those are the three primary virtues of Plato: wisdom, courage or fortitude, and temperance or self-discipline, the curb-ing of the sensual drives. In addition, Plato describes the harmo-nious balancing of these three virtues as a fourth virtue, which he calls "justice" or "righteousness" [*Gerechtigkeit*].[31]

Here you have one of the most eminent European minds of pre-Christian times describing what were regarded then as the most important qualities of human nature. Later, in the European population, courage or fortitude becomes permeated by the Christ Impulse and by what we call the ego. What appears with Plato as the virtue of courage is thereby spiritualized and thus becomes love. This is what is important, that we should see how new moral impulses enter into humanity, how what was formerly regarded as I have described today later becomes something quite different. Thus, unless we wish to fly in the face of Christian morality, we may not list the virtues as wisdom, fortitude, temperance and jus-tice, for then we could be answered: If you had all these virtues and yet had not love, never would you enter the kingdom of heaven.[32]

Let us keep in mind the epoch in which, as we have seen, an impulse of such stature was poured into humanity that wisdom and courage were spiritualized and reappeared as love. We shall continue tomorrow to consider the further development of the virtues, and in so doing we shall come to see the particular moral mission of the theosophical movement for our present time.

LECTURE THREE

May 30, 1912

In yesterday's lecture we tried to demonstrate, based on the facts presented earlier, that a foundation of morality and goodness exists within the human soul, and that only in the course of evolution from incarnation to incarnation have human beings strayed from their original instinctive tendency toward the good, and thereby allowed evil, error and immorality to enter into humanity. If this is true, however, we should be astonished that evil can exist at all, and we are impelled to ask the question: How in the course of evolution has evil become possible?

A satisfactory answer to this question can be obtained only by studying the elementary moral instruction that was given already in ancient times. Wherever instruction was given in the true sense of the Mysteries, the pupils, whose highest ideal was to penetrate gradually to complete spiritual knowledge and truth, were always obliged to work from a moral foundation. The character of the moral nature of the human being was illustrated for the pupils in a very special manner. We will describe briefly how this happened: The pupils of the Mysteries were shown that human nature can bring about destruction and harm in two directions, and that human beings are in a position to develop free will only because of this possibility of erring in two directions. Furthermore, they were shown that life can take a favorable course only when these two lines of deviation are considered to be like the two sides of a balance: as one side goes up the other side goes down, and true balance is achieved only when the crossbeam is horizontal. In this way the pupils were shown that the right conduct of a human being cannot at all be described by saying this is correct, and that is incorrect. Right conduct is achieved only through the fact that human beings are placed at every moment in the position of being pulled either to the one side or to the other—and must then themselves establish the balance.

Consider the virtue of fortitude or courage. On the one hand, human nature may swing toward recklessness, that is, toward unrestrained activity in the world with full exertion of all one's forces. That is on the one side; on the other side there is cowardice. The human being can swing, as it were, to either side, and the pupils in the Mysteries were shown that if one swings toward recklessness, one loses oneself and becomes crushed by the wheels of life. If one errs in this direction one is torn apart; on the other hand, if one errs toward the side of cowardice, one becomes hardened in oneself and thus torn away from other things and beings. One becomes a self-enclosed being whose actions cannot be brought into harmony with the whole. This was demonstrated for the pupils with regard to all human actions. Either one deviates and becomes crushed and torn apart by the objective world, thus losing oneself, or one deviates in the other direction—not just with regard to fortitude, but with any action—in such a way that one hardens within oneself. On this account, at the head of the moral code in all the Mysteries stood the important dictum: Thou must find the mean, so that through thy deeds thou dost not lose thyself to the world, nor let the world lose thee.

These are the two possibilities: Either we become lost to the world—the world seizes and overpowers us—as is the case with recklessness; or the world becomes lost to us because we harden ourselves in our egoism, as is the case with cowardice. Accordingly, the pupils in the Mysteries were told that there is no unique and fixed goodness for which one can strive; on the contrary, goodness arises solely because the human being, like a pendulum, can always swing to one side or the other, and must find the possibility of balance, the central mean, through individual inner force.

You have here everything you need in order to comprehend free will and the significance of reason and wisdom in human conduct. If it were appropriate for human beings to adhere to eternal moral principles, we would only need to adopt these principles and we could then rigidly march through life. But life is not like this. Instead, the freedom in life consists in there always being the possibility of erring in the one direction or in the other. And in this way there also arises the possibility of evil. For what is evil? Evil is what originates when we either lose ourselves to the world, or the world is lost to us. The "good" consists in avoiding both of these. Evil has become possible in the course of evolution because human beings have erred to one side or the other, and, because they did not always find the balance, were required to create karmic compensation at a future time. What cannot be achieved in one lifetime in terms of finding the mean, is achieved in the course of evolution from incarnation to incarnation. A person who errs to the one side is then obliged, perhaps in the next life, to swing to the other side and thus create compensation.[33]

What I have just told you was a golden rule in the ancient Mysteries. As is so often the case, we find an echo of this principle among the early philosophers. We find that where Aristotle speaks of virtue, he makes a statement which can be understood only if we know that what I have just told you was an ancient Mystery principle, which Aristotle received and embodied in his philosophy. That is why Aristotle gives this curious definition of virtue: Virtue is human capacity or skill guided by reason and insight, which in relation to the human being holds the mean between the too-much and the too-little. Here Aristotle gives a definition of virtue such as has not been achieved by any subsequent philosophy. Because Aristotle had the tradition from the Mysteries, he could find the precise truth. This, then, is the famous mean, which one must keep to in order to be virtuous, in order for moral power to stream through the world.[34]

We can now also answer the question of why morality exists. For what happens when morality is absent? What happens when the too-much or the too-little holds sway, when either the human being is lost to and crushed by the world, or the world is lost to the human being? In each case, something is always destroyed. Everything evil or immoral is a process of destruction, and the moment we realize that when we do evil we cannot do otherwise than destroy and eliminate something from the world, in that moment we are overwhelmed by the impulse of goodness. The task of the theosophical movement, which is now only beginning to enter the world, is to show how all evil brings about a destructive process that eliminates something necessary in the world.

If we now adhere to the principle that we have just enunciated, then what we know about the nature of the human being from our theosophical world-conception, leads us to a specific elaboration of the nature of goodness, as well as of evil. We know that the sentient-soul was chiefly developed in the ancient Chaldean epoch, in the third post-Atlantean cultural epoch.

People today have little notion what this epoch of evolution was like, for in external history one can reach back little farther than Egyptian times. We know too that the mind-soul or heart-soul developed during the fourth epoch, the Greco-Latin epoch, and that now in our epoch we are developing the consciousness-soul. The spirit-self will be developed in the sixth epoch.[35]

Let us now ask: In what way can the sentient-soul stray from the good, either to the one side or to the other? The sentient-soul is what enables the human being to experience the world of objects, to come into a relationship with the objects rather than passing them by unknowingly. We find the one way in which the sentient-soul can stray when we ask ourselves, What is it that enables us to have a relationship with our surroundings? It is what we may call our interest in things. This word "interest" expresses something that in a moral sense is extremely significant. It is much more important to bear in mind the moral significance of interest than to devote oneself to a multitude of moral axioms, which may be beautiful or perhaps also trivial and sanctimonious. Our moral impulses are in fact never guided better than when we take proper interest in objects or beings. Please think about this. Because we spoke in yesterday's lecture of the deeper meaning of love, I will not be misunderstood when I say that even the usual, oft-repeated saying of "love, love, and love again," cannot replace the moral impulse that lies behind the little word "interest."

Let us suppose we have a child before us. What is the precondition for our devoting ourselves to this child, what is the precondition for our being able to help this child? The precondition is that we take an interest in it. The human soul is unhealthy if it withdraws from something in which it should take an interest. The more one gets beyond mere preaching to the real foundations of morality, the more one will recognize that in a moral sense the impulse of interest is an especially golden impulse. When we extend our interests, when we find opportunity to enter with understanding into the objects and beings of the world, our inner forces are called forth. If we take an interest in a person, our compassion is called forth in an appropriate manner. If we as theosophists set ourselves the task of increasingly extending our interests, of increasingly widening our horizons, this will promote the universal brotherhood of humanity.[36] Progress is not made by the mere preaching of universal love, but by the extension of our interest further and further, so that we increasingly come to be interested in and to understand people with widely different temperaments and personalities, with widely different racial and national characteristics, with widely different religious and philosophical views. Right understanding, right interest, calls forth from the soul the right moral conduct.

Here too we must hold the balance between two extremes. One extreme is apathy, which is the cause of tremendous moral catastrophes in the world. Apathetic persons are indifferent to the world; they live only in themselves and stubbornly insist on their own viewpoint. In a moral sense, this insistence on a viewpoint is never something good. What is important is that we be open to all that is around us. Apathy removes us from the world, whereas interest places us within it. Through our apathy the world loses us, and we become immoral. Apathy and lack of interest in the world are to the highest degree immoral.

Theosophy, however, is something that stimulates the mind and helps us to comprehend and absorb the spiritual. Just as warmth comes forth when we light a fire in a stove, so interest in human beings and all other beings arises when we assimilate theosophical truths. Wisdom is the fuel for interest. Although it may not immediately be obvious, we can say that when we study those more remote theosophical teachings about Saturn, Sun and Moon, or about karma and so forth, that these arouse in us this interest in the world. It is truly so that interest is what arises as the transformed product of theosophical knowledge, whereas materialistic knowledge gives rise to what is unfortunately so very prevalent today, what in radical fashion we must designate as apathy, and which if it alone were present, would necessarily cause tremendous harm.

Just notice the way many people go through the world, how they may meet other people but do not really get to know them because they are shut up in themselves. How often do we find that two people have been friends for a long time and then suddenly come to a breach. This is because their friendship was based on a materialistic foundation, and for a long time they had not noticed that they had mutually unsympathetic character traits. Very few people today have a clear sense for what speaks from one human being to another human being. But this is just what theosophy should bring about; it should broaden us so that we acquire a clear sense and an open soul for everything human around us, so that we do not pass through the world apathetically but with proper interest.

We also avoid the other extreme here, inasmuch as we distinguish between genuine interest and false interest, and thereby keep to the mean. Throwing ourselves immediately into the arms of everything we meet is not genuine interest but wanton loss of self. If we do this, we lose ourselves to the world. Through apathy the world loses us, through blind passion we surrender ourselves to the world. Through healthy interest we keep firmly to the mean, to the state of balance.

In the third post-Atlantean epoch of civilization, the Chaldaic-Egyptian epoch, the majority of humanity on earth still had the power to hold the balance between apathy and passionate, beclouded surrender to the world; this is what in ancient times, and even still with Plato and Aristotle, was called "wisdom." The people regarded this, however, as the gift of superhuman beings, for in those times the ancient impulses of wisdom were still active. Consequently, from the point of view of moral impulses, the third post-Atlantean epoch may be called the epoch of instinctive wisdom. We may thus also experience the truth of what was said last year in my Copenhagen lectures, which are now available in the booklet *The Spiritual Guidance of the Individual and Humanity*.[37] There it was described—though for quite different reasons—how in the third post-Atlantean epoch humanity still stood closer to the divine-spiritual powers. And what allowed this closer connection, was the instinctive wisdom.

Thus, in those times, the power to find the mean between apathy and passionate surrender was a divine endowment. The mean or balance was still maintained through external traditions and customs. The complete intermingling of peoples that began with the Great Migrations in the fourth post-Atlantean epoch had not yet begun; humanity was still divided into tribes and clans. In these the interests were naturally and wisely regulated; the interests were active enough for the right moral impulses to appear, while the existence of consanguinity within the tribes held the passions in check. Even in our time, you will admit that interest develops most easily where blood relationship or genealogy is involved. There too, what one calls blind passion is also not present. Because during the Chaldaic-Egyptian epoch people lived in limited territories, the wisdom-filled mean was easily maintained.

The meaning of human evolution, however, is that what was originally instinctive and divine should gradually disappear, that human beings should gradually become independent of the divine-spiritual powers. Hence we see already in the fourth post-Atlantean epoch—the Greco-Latin epoch—that not only the philosophers Plato and Aristotle, but also Greek public opinion regarded wisdom as something to be acquired; it was no longer a divine legacy but had to be striven for. The first virtue for Plato is wisdom, and according to him, anyone who does not strive for wisdom is immoral.

We are now in the fifth post-Atlantean epoch. We are still far from the time when the wisdom instinctively implanted in humanity as a divine impulse will be fully raised into consciousness. Hence in our time it is especially possible for people to stray in both of the directions we have indicated. This is why it is especially necessary to counteract these great dangers by means of a spiritual world view, so that what humanity once had as instinctive wisdom can now become conscious wisdom. This is the purpose of the theosophical movement. The unconscious human soul once received wisdom from the gods as something instinctive, but now the truths about the cosmos and about human evolution have to be acquired consciously. The customs and social mores in ancient times conformed to the thoughts of the gods, and we regard theosophy rightly if we regard it as the investigation of those divine thoughts. In the past they came instinctively; today we have to study them and raise them to consciousness. In this sense we have to regard theosophy as something divine. We have to consider with reverence that the thoughts conveyed to us through theosophy are really something divine, something that we are privileged to think, since they are a reflection of the divine world order. When we relate to theosophy in this manner, we realize that this knowledge has been given to us so that we can carry out our mission. Tremendous truths are disclosed to us if we study what has been imparted concerning the earth's evolution through the stages of "Saturn," "Sun" and "Moon," concerning the development of the different races, concerning reincarnation, and so on.[38] But we only take the right attitude to this if we say to ourselves: The thoughts we are pursuing are the thoughts according to which the gods have guided evolution. We are thinking the evolution of the gods. If we truly comprehend this, then we cannot help but be overwhelmed by something that is deeply moral. We then say to ourselves: "In the past people had instinctive wisdom from the gods. The gods gave them the wisdom according to which they had fashioned the world, and this enabled the people to act morally. Now in theosophy we acquire the wisdom consciously. Therefore we can also be confident that this wisdom will transform itself in us into moral impulses, so that what we are absorbing are not just theosophical truths, but moral impulses as well."

Now, what is the nature of these moral impulses that we are absorbing? We touch here on a point in evolution whose attainment the theosophist can certainly foresee, and whose deep moral significance indeed should be foreseen. We touch on a point that is far removed from what is prevalent today, namely, what Plato still called the ideal of wisdom. Since he used a word that was commonplace when wisdom still lived instinctively within people, it will be good if we replace it with a different word. Because we have become more individualized and have distanced ourselves from the divine, it will be good if we replace it with the word "truthfulness." We must learn to feel the full significance of this word. With respect to morality, this will be one of the effects of the theosophical world outlook. People will learn to experience truthfulness through theosophy.

The theosophists of today will learn how very necessary it is to feel the moral dimension of truthfulness. Nowadays one still talks about truthfulness, but due to the materialism of our age, the general culture is far removed from experiencing the moral need for this. Today this cannot be otherwise. Truth is something that contemporary culture must necessarily be severely lacking in, because contemporary culture maintains a different trait. I ask you, do people still feel anything today when they read something in a newspaper or somewhere else and then learn later that what they had read simply wasn't true? I ask you to ponder this seriously. One cannot say one meets this at every turn, one must say one meets it at every quarter turn! Untruthfulness has become a trait of our present cultural epoch, wherever modern life extends. It is impossible to say that truthfulness is characteristic of our epoch.

Nowadays, if you confront people whom you know have written or said something untrue, you will find as a rule that they have no feeling at all for the wrongness of this. They will immediately respond, "Well, I said it in good faith." Theosophists should not regard this as moral. People must increasingly learn to come to the point where they know whether what they assert really happened. In other words, one may say or report something only after one has felt and acted on the obligation to test with all the means at one's disposal whether it is actually so. Only when one accepts this obligation, can truthfulness be experienced as moral impulse. Then people will no longer say, after having placed something incorrect into the world, "That's the way I thought it was, I said it in good faith." They will learn that one is obliged, not merely to say what one believes is correct, but to say only what one knows to be true and correct. In this respect, a radical change must gradually enter into our culture. The rapid pace of life, the craving for sensations, everything that is a consequence of a materialistic age, all these are opponents of truthfulness. In the area of morality, theosophy will be an educator of humanity to the duty of truthfulness.

It is not my task today to discuss to what degree truthfulness has already been realized within the Theosophical Society, but I will say that what has been expressed today must in principle be a high theosophical ideal. The moral development within the theosophical movement will have enough to do if the moral ideal of truthfulness is felt and thought through in all directions.

This moral ideal of truthfulness will be what produces virtue in the sentient-soul in the right manner.[39]

The second part of the soul that we have to speak of in theosophy is what we usually call the mind-soul or heart-soul [*Verstandes- oder Gemütsseele*]. You know that this came into its own particularly during the fourth post-Atlantean cultural epoch, the Greco-Latin epoch. We have already described the virtue that is particularly decisive for this part of the soul—it is courage, fortitude, bravery. Its extremes are recklessness and cowardice. Bravery, courage or fortitude is the mean between recklessness and cowardice. The German word *Gemüt* expresses already in its sound that it is related to the part of the soul that is "full of courage" [*mutvoll*], the part that is full of strength and force. This was also the second or middle virtue for Plato and Aristotle. In the fourth post-Atlantean epoch this virtue was still present in people as a divine legacy, whereas wisdom as something instinctive was still present only through the third post-Atlantean epoch. As you will have gathered from the first lecture, instinctive fortitude and courage existed as a divine legacy among the people who met the northward expansion of Christianity during the fourth cultural epoch. Just as wisdom-filled insight into the secrets of the starry worlds was present among the Chaldeans as a divine endowment or inspiration, so were fortitude and courage present among the Greeks and Romans, and also among the peoples who later took up the spread of Christianity. Instinctive courage was lost later than instinctive wisdom.

If now in the fifth post-Atlantean epoch we look around us, we see that we are in the same position, in regard to fortitude and courage, as the Greeks were to the Chaldeans and Egyptians in regard to wisdom. We look back at something that was a divine endowment in the epoch immediately preceding ours, and that in a certain way we must strive for again. But the two previous lectures have shown us that in connection with this effort a certain transformation must take place. We saw the divine endowment, which had a more external character as fortitude and courage, became transformed in Francis of Assisi. We saw this transformation as the result of an inner moral force, which we recognized yesterday as the force of the Christ Impulse. Genuine love is brought about by the transformation of courage and fortitude. This genuine love, however, must be guided by the other virtue, by genuine interest in the being toward whom we direct our love. In *Timon of Athens*, Shakespeare shows how even love and kindheartedness can cause harm if manifested too passionately, if they appear merely as a part of human nature without being guided by wisdom or truthfulness. Shakespeare portrays a personality who completely squanders his possessions. Generosity is a virtue, but in Shakespeare's play we see that what is squandered produces nothing but parasites.[40]

Thus we must say: Just as the ancient fortitude and courage were guided by the European Brahmans in the Mystery Centers, by the wise leaders who kept themselves hidden in the background, so also in human nature must the virtue of love be harmoniously guided by interest. The interest that brings us into relation with the outer world in the right way must lead and guide us when we turn our love to the outer world. This may also be seen in the characteristic but radical example of Francis of Assisi. The compassion and pity that Francis of Assisi had was not the sort that easily becomes obtrusive or offensive. People who smother other people with their compassion are not always actuated by the best moral impulses, and many people will not accept anything given out of pity. To approach someone with understanding, however, is not offensive. Under certain circumstances, pity is something that must be rejected; but no healthy person can reject being approached with understanding. Thus, if a person's actions are in accord with this understanding, these actions cannot be faulted either.

It is this understanding that can guide us with respect to the second virtue, the virtue of compassion and love. Through the Christ Impulse, this has become the virtue of the mind-soul or heart-soul. This virtue can be characterized as human love that is accompanied by human understanding.

Compassion is the virtue that will produce in future the most beautiful and glorious fruits in human communities, for in a certain way this compassion and love will arise quite naturally as a feeling in those who truly grasp the Christ Impulse. And it is exactly through the theosophical comprehension of the Christ Impulse that this will become a natural feeling.

Christ has descended into earthly evolution through the Mystery of Golgotha. His impulses, His activities are here, are everywhere. Why did He descend to this earth? He descended in order that through what He can give the world, evolution may go forward in the right way and fulfill itself. If we now destroy something as a result of immorality, as a result of passing by our fellow human beings without interest, then we take something away from the world into which the Christ Impulse has entered. Hence we directly destroy a part of the Christ Impulse, now that it is here. But if we give to the world what can be given through creative virtue, then we augment the world. We augment it simply through our giving. Not for nothing has it often been said that although Christ was first crucified on Golgotha, He continues to be crucified again and again through human deeds. Because Christ has entered into earthly evolution through the Deed on Golgotha, everything immoral that we do, every instance of lovelessness and apathy, contributes to the suffering and pain inflicted on Him. For this reason it has repeatedly been said: Christ is continually crucified as long as immorality, lovelessness and apathy exist; since the Christ Impulse has permeated the world, it is this that bears the suffering.

Just as it is true that through destructive evil we withdraw something from the Christ Impulse, and as it were continue the Crucifixion on Golgotha, so too is it true that where we perform deeds of love, we help to bring the Christ Impulse to life. "Verily I say unto you, inasmuch as ye have done it unto one of the least of these my brethren, ye have done it unto me"[41]—this is the most momentous testimony of love, and this testimony must become the most profound moral impulse, once it is theosophically understood. We do this when we approach our fellow human beings with understanding and offer them something in our deeds or our attitude that comes from an understanding of their being. Our attitude toward our fellow human beings is our attitude toward the Christ Impulse itself.

It is a powerful moral impulse, a real foundation for morality, to feel: "The Mystery of Golgotha was enacted for all human beings, and from there an impulse has spread into the whole world. If you encounter other people, try to understand them in all their differences, whether it be of race, color, nationality, religious

belief or world view. When you meet them and do this or that to
them, you do it to the Christ. In the present stage of earthly evolution, what you do to your fellow human beings, you do also to
the Christ." This statement—"I say unto you, inasmuch as ye have
done it to one of these my brethren, ye have done it unto me"—
will become a potent moral impulse for those who understand the
fundamental meaning of the Mystery of Golgotha.

Thus we can say: As the gods of pre-Christian times gave
humanity instinctive wisdom, instinctive courage and fortitude, so
does love stream down from the symbol of the Cross—love that is
built upon the mutual interest between one human being and
another. Through this the Christ Impulse will work in a mighty
way in the world. When the day comes that the Brahman understands and loves not only the Brahman, the Pariah the Pariah, the
Jew the Jew, the Christian the Christian, but when the Jew understands and has compassion for the Christian as a human being,
and the Pariah for the Brahman, the American for the Asian, then
one will know how deeply Christian it is to say: There must be
brotherliness among human beings without regard to outer con-
fession. We should give little heed to what otherwise unites us; we
should care less for father, mother, brother, sister, even our own
life, than for what speaks from one human soul to another. "They
who in this sense do not give little heed to the differentiation, to
what hinders the Christ Impulse that equalizes the differences
among human beings, they cannot be my disciples." That is the
impulse of love that radiates from the Mystery of Golgotha,
which in this regard we experience as a renewal of what was once
given to humanity as original virtue.

Now we still have to consider what may be called the virtue of
the consciousness-soul: temperance or self-discipline. In the
fourth post-Atlantean cultural epoch these virtues were still

instinctive. Plato and Aristotle spoke of them as the chief virtues of the consciousness-soul, inasmuch as they considered them to be the mean of what exists in the consciousness-soul.[42] The consciousness-soul arises when the human being becomes conscious of the outer world by means of the physical body. The physical body is the primary instrument of the consciousness-soul, and it is through the physical body that the human being comes to full self-consciousness. The physical body must therefore be maintained; if the human physical body were not maintained, the mission of the earth could not be fulfilled. But here too there is a limit. If people used all of their forces only to satisfy themselves, they would shut themselves off from the world; the world would lose them. On the other hand, people who deny themselves everything, increasingly weaken themselves and are eventually crushed by the external world process. People who overtax the forces allotted to the human being, are taken up by the world process and lose themselves in the world. The body that has evolved to serve the consciousness-soul can be crushed by the world, or the human being can come to lose contact with the world. Temperance is the virtue that enables the human being to avoid both of these extremes. Temperance is neither asceticism nor self-indulgence, but the proper mean between the two. This is the virtue of the consciousness-soul.

With regard to this virtue, we have not yet progressed beyond the instinctive standpoint. A little reflection will convince you that, on the whole, people are very much given to sampling the two extremes; they tend to swing back and forth between them. If you disregard the few who are endeavoring already now to bring some consciousness into this area, you will find that most people live very much according to a pattern, which in central Europe is often described by saying: There are people in Berlin who indulge in various delicacies and treats throughout the winter, and then in summer go to Carlsbad, where by means of the other extreme they correct the harm they have done to themselves over the winter. You see, the balance tips first to the one side and then to the other. That is a radical case, but even if it doesn't always happen to that degree, this alternation between indulgence and deprivation is present everywhere. That is clear enough. The people themselves cause the excess to one side, and then let their doctors prescribe a so-called withdrawal program—that is to say, the other extreme—in order to repair the damage.

You see from this that in this area people are still in a very instinctive condition, and that we must say it is a kind of divine legacy that people still have an instinctive feeling not to do too much in the one direction nor in the other. But just as the other instinctive qualities have been lost, so too will this one be lost in the transition from the fifth post-Atlantean epoch to the sixth. This will be lost as a natural legacy—and now you can judge how much theosophy will have to contribute toward developing more and more consciousness in this area.

Very few theosophists today, even those who are more advanced, realize that theosophy is the remedy to bring about the right consciousness in this area too. When theosophy develops further in this area, something will come about that I can only describe in the following way: People will gradually have more and more longing for the great spiritual truths. Though theosophy may be mocked today, it will not always be so. It will spread, it will conquer all the outer opposition and everything else that still hinders it, and theosophists will not be content just to preach about universal love. People will understand that one cannot assimilate theosophy in a day any more than one can eat enough in a day for one's whole life, and that it is therefore necessary to assimilate ever more from theosophy. Within the theosophical movement people will less and less often say: These are our fundamental principles, and if we have these principles, then we are true theosophists. Instead, what will increasingly spread is the feeling of always standing within a community, of communally experiencing the vitality of theosophy.

Now, when people work over in themselves the characteristic thoughts, the characteristic feelings and impulses that come from theosophical wisdom, what takes place? As you know, theosophists can never have a materialistic world view; they have just the opposite. A materialist would say: If a person has these or those thoughts, then the molecules or atoms of the brain are in motion, and because this motion is going on, the person has the thoughts. The thoughts emerge from the brain like a thin smoke, or like the flame from a candle. That is the materialistic view. The theosophical view is exactly the opposite. There it is the thoughts, the experiences in the soul, that bring the brain or nervous system into motion. The manner in which our brain moves depends on the thoughts we think. That is just the opposite of what the materialists believe. If you wish to know how people's brains are constituted, you must investigate what thoughts they had; for just as written characters are nothing else than the result of the thoughts, so too are the motions of the brain nothing else than the result of the thoughts.

Mustn't we then also come to say that people's brains will be affected differently when they are thinking theosophical thoughts than when they are in a club playing cards? Different processes occur in their soul when they follow theosophical thoughts than when they are in a card club or watching a movie. Nothing in the human organism is isolated, everything is interrelated; one thing acts on another. Our thoughts act on the brain and nervous system, and this is connected to our entire organism. Though most people are not yet aware of it, once the inherited tendencies that are still in our bodies are overcome, the following will take place. Thoughts will pass from the brain to the stomach, and the result will be that certain things that still taste good to people today will no longer taste good to those who have absorbed theosophical thoughts. The thoughts that theosophists take in are divine thoughts. These act upon the whole organism in such a manner that what is good for it will also taste good. What is not good for the organism will be smelled and found unsympathetic. This is an unusual perspective, a perspective that some will indeed call materialistic, but it is just the opposite. This kind of appetite—whereby one loves and prefers to eat certain things, and hates and will not eat others—this will emerge as a consequence of theosophical work. You can also test this on yourself, if you notice that you perhaps have an aversion to certain things, which you did not have before you encountered theosophy.

Such things will become more and more common if people work selflessly on their higher development, so that the world can receive from them what is right. Only one must not play hide-and-seek with the words "selflessness" and "egoism." In fact, it is very easy to misuse these words. It is not pure selflessness when someone says, "I only want to work in and for the world; what does my own spiritual development matter? I only want to work, not strive egoistically. . . ." It is not egoism when people develop themselves, because in fact they thereby make themselves more suited to actively partake in the further development of the world. Neglecting one's own further development renders one unfit for the world; one withdraws one's power from the world. Here too we must do the right thing, so that what the Godhead intended for us may also come to manifestation.

Through theosophy a human race will develop—or rather, a nucleus of humanity will develop[43]—that does not take temperance as a guiding ideal merely out of instinct. It will have a conscious sympathy for what makes the human being a worthy building stone of the divine world order, and a conscious aversion to what destroys the human being as a building stone of the world order.

So we see that moral impulses are present also where human beings develop themselves, and in this way we find instinctive temperance transformed into what we might call "life-wisdom" [*Lebensweisheit*]. The ideal of life-wisdom, which will be a demand of the next, the sixth post-Atlantean epoch, will also be the virtue that Plato called "justice"—the harmonious accord of the virtues. Since the virtues have somewhat shifted in humanity, what was regarded as "justice" in pre-Christian times has changed as well. In those times the harmonization was not brought about by this sort of individualized virtue; such harmonization was a distant future ideal.[44]

We have seen that courage transformed itself into the moral impulse of love. We have also seen that wisdom became truthfulness, the virtue that can place the human being worthily and properly into everyday life. But if we want to come to truthfulness with regard to the spiritual world, how can we do this? We come to outer truthfulness—to what glows in our sentient-soul as virtue—through right understanding, through right interest. What then is interest with regard to the spiritual world? If we want to meet the physical world or, to start with, a human being, then we must open ourselves to the nature of this being. But how do we open ourselves with regard to the spiritual world? We can do this if we develop a very particular kind of feeling, a feeling that also developed in history when the old instinctive wisdom had sunk into the depths of the soul. It is the feeling that we often find the Greeks describing with the dictum: All philosophy begins with wonder, with astonishment.[45] When wonder and astonishment are placed at the beginning of our relationship to the supersensible world, this is also the expression of something essentially moral. The great phenomena of the world do not at first call forth much wonder from uncultivated persons. It is exactly through spiritual development that people come to discover the riddles in everyday phenomena, to get a hint of the spirituality behind them. It is wonder that leads our souls upward into the spiritual realms so that we can come to know them, and we can only come to know them if our souls are attracted by the entities to be known. This attraction is what is brought about by wonder and astonishment and also by faith. It is always wonder and astonishment that guide us to the supersensible, and at the same time this is what one usually calls faith. Faith, wonder, astonishment are three forces of the soul that lead us beyond the ordinary world.[46]

If we encounter someone and are filled with wonder and awe, then we are seeking to understand them. Through understanding a person's being we arrive at the virtue of brotherly love, and we can best actualize this virtue if we have approached people with awe. Then we shall see that awe is something that we must bring toward every person. If we do this, we will come to be ever more truthful. We will feel an obligation toward truth. We will sense ourselves drawing closer to the spiritual world, and through knowing this world we shall reacquire the spiritual wisdom that has sunk into the unconscious realms of the soul. Only after the spiritual wisdom had disappeared did the saying arise that philosophy begins with wonder and astonishment. This can make clear to you that wonder and astonishment first entered evolution at the time the Christ Impulse came into the world.

Since we have already spoken about the second virtue, about love, let us now turn our attention to what is presently still instinctive temperance, but which we have said will in future become life-wisdom. With temperance and with life-wisdom we are concerned with ourselves. We act, as it were, in such a way that through our actions in the world we take care of ourselves. For this reason it is necessary that we also acquire a more objective standard.

In Greek times, in the fourth post-Atlantean epoch, something arose that I have often spoken about in other settings, namely conscience.[47] One can clearly trace how in the old Greek dramas such as those of Aeschylus, the Erinyes or Furies play a role that with Euripides is transformed into conscience.[48] From this we see that what we call conscience did not at all exist in earlier times. Conscience is something that stands there as a standard for our actions when we go too far in our demands or in seeking our own advantage. It acts as a standard that places itself between our sympathies and antipathies. We thereby acquire something that is more objective, as it were, something that acts more toward the outside, compared to the virtues of truthfulness, love and life-wisdom.

Love stands here in the middle and acts as something that must permeate and regulate all of life. It must regulate all of social life, and must also work regulatively on the inner impulses we have developed.[49] What we have developed as truthfulness, on the other hand, will manifest as faith in spiritual knowledge. And life-wisdom—that which applies to ourselves—we must still experience as a divine-spiritual regulator, one that leads us securely along the path of the mean, just as conscience does.

If we had time, it would be very easy to answer the various objections that could be raised at this point. Some people, for instance, would deny that conscience and wonder are qualities

that have appeared only gradually within humanity, and instead
maintain that they are eternal characteristics of human nature.[50]
In fact, however, they are not, and those who maintain that they
are, demonstrate only that they do not know the relevant facts.
People will increasingly come to recognize that in ancient times
human beings had not descended so far toward the physical plane
and thus still retained a connection with the divine impulses.
They were in a condition that will be reacquired consciously when
human beings become governed by truthfulness, love and the art
of life[51] in regard to matters of the physical plane, and when in
regard to spiritual knowledge they become governed by faith in
the supersensible world. This need not be a faith that leads
directly into the supersensible world; but ultimately it will transform itself into spiritual knowledge. And as it is with faith, so too
is it with love that works outwardly. And conscience is what will
work regulatively into the consciousness-soul.[52]

Faith, love, conscience—these three forces will be the three
stars of the moral forces that will enter into human souls particularly through theosophy. A moral perspective on the future can
open itself only to those who think of these three virtues as
becoming ever more enhanced. Theosophists will regard moral
life in the light of these virtues, and these virtues will be construc-
tive forces for the future.[53]

We shall conclude by briefly touching on something that
could be more securely founded if lengthier explanations were
possible. We are aware that the Christ Impulse entered human
evolution through the Mystery of Golgotha. We know that with
the Baptism in the Jordan, a human organism—consisting of
physical body, etheric body and astral body—received the ego-
impulse from above, as the Christ Impulse. This Christ Impulse
entered as the ego of Christ and was then absorbed by the earth

and flowed into earthly culture. We know too, that Jesus of Nazareth retained the physical body, etheric body and astral body; the Christ Impulse had been like the ego within them. On Golgotha, Jesus of Nazareth separated himself from the Christ Impulse, which then flowed into earthly evolution. The evolution of this impulse signifies the evolution of the earth itself.[54]

Please treat with all seriousness the things that I mention repeatedly so that they may be better understood. We have often heard that the world is maya or illusion, but gradually we must advance to the truth, to the reality of this outer world. The evolution of the earth is basically a process in which in the second half—the half we are in—everything that formed itself in the first half now dissolves itself, so that everything physical we see around us will fall away from human evolution, just as the human physical body falls away at death. What then still remains? one might ask. What remains are the forces, the real forces that were incorporated into human beings through the process of earthly evolution. And the *most* real impulse in this process is what flowed into earthly evolution through the Christ Impulse. Initially, however, this Christ Impulse cannot find anything on earth with which to clothe itself. In the further course of earth evolution, therefore, it must receive such clothing. When the earth has reached its culmination, then, as Adam was the first human being, so will the fully developed Christ be the "last" human being, around whom humanity in its manifoldness will have grouped itself.[55]

The words—"I say unto you, inasmuch as ye have done it unto one of these my brethren, ye have done it unto me"—contain a significant clue for us. What is it that has been done for the Christ? Deeds that are done out of the Christ Impulse, or under the influence of conscience, or under the influence of faith that is in accord with knowledge, these separate themselves out from earthly life, and, inasmuch as through moral deeds and attitudes one gives something to one's brothers, one also gives to the Christ. I will express it as a sort of formula: Everything in the way of forces that we create through deeds of faith and trust, through deeds done out of wonder and astonishment, is something that is given over to the Christ-ego and that envelops the Christ like a sheath comparable to our astral body. We build the astral body of the Christ-ego Impulse through all moral deeds done out of wonder, trust, awe, faith—in short, through everything that paves the way to supersensible knowledge. Through all these deeds we also foster love. This is entirely in accord with the words, "I say unto you, inasmuch as ye have done it unto one of these my brethren, ye have done it unto me." Through our deeds of love we build the etheric body of the Christ. And by means of what is created in the world through the impulse of conscience, we build for the Christ Impulse that which corresponds to the human physical body. When the earth eventually reaches its goal, when human beings understand the moral impulses through which all goodness occurs, then will the Christ Impulse, which entered into human evolution like an ego, be liberated. It will be ensheathed by an astral body built up through faith and through all deeds of wonder and astonishment, by an etheric body built up through deeds of love, and by something like a physical body, built up through deeds of conscience.[56]

The future evolution of humanity will take place through the cooperation of human moral impulses with the Christ Impulse. Looking toward the future, we see humanity as a great organic structure. As human beings are able to integrate their actions into this organism, and through their actions create its sheaths, humanity will have prepared in the course of earth evolution the foundation for a mighty community which can be thoroughly permeated by the Christ Impulse.

In this way we see that morality does not need to be preached but can indeed be founded if one shows what really happens, and what really has happened, and what makes these things true as sensitive people feel them to be. It is always particularly touching to see how Goethe, after having lost his friend Duke Karl August, wrote a lengthy letter in which he described all manner of things, and how he then—this was in 1828, just three and a half years before his own death—put down a wonderfully curious sentence: "The world of reason should be regarded as a great immortal individual, which continually produces what is necessary and thereby elevates itself to become master even of the accidental."[57] How else could we make such a thought more concrete than by imagining this individual actively and creatively among us, and by thinking of ourselves as actively and creatively united with it? Through the Mystery of Golgotha the greatest Individual entered into human evolution, and by consciously conducting their lives as has been described, human beings will array themselves around the Christ Impulse, so that a kind of covering will be formed around this central Being.

There is indeed much more that we could say about virtue from the perspective of theosophy. We could, for instance, make an extensive and important study of truthfulness and its connection with karma. Through theosophy the idea of karma will increasingly have to enter into human evolution. People will increasingly have to learn to regard and conduct their lives in such a way that their virtues correspond with their karma. People will have to learn through the idea of karma that they may not repudiate their earlier deeds with their later deeds. A certain consequentiality in life, a readiness to take on the consequences of what one has done, will have to emerge in human evolution. When one looks more closely, one sees how far removed from this people still are. Although it is well known that personal development depends on the deeds one does, once the consequence of a deed is no longer apparent, people still do what they would in fact only be allowed to do if they had not done the first deed. A greater feeling of responsibility for one's actions, a greater awareness of karma, that is what a study of this sort might yield.

Nevertheless, you will still be able to discover much for yourselves in the guidelines given in these three lectures. You will find, for example, how fruitful these ideas can be when you develop them further. As human beings pass through repeated incarnations during the remainder of earth evolution, they face the task of producing the balance, the middle condition, with respect to the virtues we have described; they face the task of rectifying through their own free will everything that they have neglected in the one direction or in the other, so that gradually the goal may be reached of clothing the Christ Impulse.

Thus we see before us not merely the abstract ideal of universal human brotherhood—which indeed may also receive a strong impulse if it is founded on theosophy—but we see that there is something real within our earth evolution, an impulse that came into the world through the Mystery of Golgotha. And we see too that we must work on the sentient-soul, the mind-soul and the consciousness-soul in order for this ideal Being to become real, and in order for us to become united with this Being as with a great immortal Individual.

The thought that the only possibility for further evolution, for achieving the earth's mission, exists in forming a whole with this great Individual, this leads to the following moral axiom: What you do as though it concerned only yourself, this separates you from this great Individual, and you thereby destroy something; but what you do to build up this great immortal Individual, as we have described, this furthers the life and development of the entire world organism.

We need only place these two thoughts before us to see that they do not just preach morality but give it a foundation. The thought that you are destroying through your deeds that which you ought to build up is terrifying and horrible and suppresses all contrary desires. On the other hand, the thought that you are building up this immortal Individual, that you are making yourself a member of this immortal Individual, this fires one to good deeds, to intensive moral impulses. Here morality is not just preached, but thoughts are indicated that can become the foundation for morality, that can themselves become moral impulses.

The more that truthfulness is cultivated, the more rapidly will such morality enter theosophical views and attitudes toward life. I have taken it as my task to speak of this in these three lectures. Although some things could only be alluded to, your own souls will be able to extend the thoughts we have touched on in these three evenings. In this way we shall also be united over all the earth. When we meet together in common study—as we have done now as theosophists of northern and central Europe—and then allow the thoughts aroused in us to resound further, this is the very best way to help theosophy establish real spiritual life at the present time. Though we must now part ways, we know that we are most united with each other in our theosophical thoughts, and this knowledge is at the same time a moral impulse. To know that one is united by the same ideals with others who are often distant in space, but with whom one can meet from time to time on special occasions, this is a stronger moral impulse than always being together.

At the end of these lectures my soul too is filled with this conception of our common endeavor, and if this is understood in the right light, I am convinced that theosophical life that unfolds in this way will also become spiritually grounded . With these thoughts and these feelings I wish to express my farewell and bring our studies to a close.

Notes

These lectures were recorded in shorthand by an unidentified stenographer. The editors of the German edition were Paul Jenny and Johann Waeger. Their editorial notes were extensively supplemented for this English edition by the translator.

Works of Rudolf Steiner are cited in English translation whenever possible. Complete publication information appears in the References section (pp. 87–92). Some of the extracts in the Notes have been newly translated.

LECTURE ONE

1. During these lectures Steiner does not, in fact, explicitly speak further about his impulse for discussing the topic of morality. Compare, however, the Translator's Introduction.
2. Saint John the Evangelist: 1st century A.D. Writer of the fourth Gospel, the Epistles of John, and the book of Revelation. On his precept of love, see: *The Golden Legend of Jacobus de Voragine*, p. 63.
3. Arthur Schopenhauer: 1788-1860. German philosopher. The quotation is from "Preisschrift über die Grundlagen der Moral."

4.   As used by Steiner, "occultism" refers to the sacred wisdom that
     has been cultivated through the ages in esoteric schools known as
     "Mystery Centers" or "Mysteries." When translated into concep-
     tual form, this wisdom becomes "theosophy" (also "anthropos-
     ophy" or "spiritual science").

5.   Steiner distinguishes seven "cultural epochs" within the "post-
     Atlantean age" (the age that began after the Deluge destroyed the
     continent of Atlantis [cf. note 14]). The chronology of these seven
     epochs is roughly as follows:

Ancient Indian	8th to 6th millennium B.C.
Ancient Persian	6th to 3rd millennium B.C.
Chaldaic–Egyptian	3rd to 1st millennium B.C.
Greco–Latin	8th cent. B.C. to 15th cent. A.D.
Fifth (present)	15th cent. A.D. to 4th mill. A.D.
Sixth	4th to 6th millennium A.D.
Seventh	6th to 8th millennium A.D.

For a description of the individual epochs, see Steiner: *Occult Science: An Outline*, chap. 4 (p. 201 ff.) and chap. 6.

6.   Hartmann von Aue: 1160?–1213. Middle High German min-
     nesinger and epic poet. His epic poem *Der arme Heinrich* was
     written between 1190 and 1197.

7.   Saint Francis of Assisi: 1182–1226. Founder of the Franciscan
     Order of monks.

8.   Saint Hildegard of Bingen: 1098–1179. Abbess at the Benedic-
     tine convent at Rupertsberg by Bingen in Germany.

9.   The Akasha Chronicle is a "living script" of the spiritual history
     of the world. For further details, see Steiner: *Cosmic Memory*,
     chap. 2; and June 25, 1909, *The Gospel of St. John and Its Relation to
     the Other Gospels*, lec. 2.

10. This dream-vision is described by St. Hildegard in a letter to the
     priest Werner of Kirchheim:

     When, in the year 1170 after the incarnation of the Divine, I lay in
     my sickbed for a long time, I saw, while I was awake in both body
     and spirit, the form of a very beautiful lady. She was a woman of
     exquisite charm, so attractive in her loveliness and possessed of such
     beauty that the human spirit was unable to comprehend it. Her
     form towered above the Earth all the way up to the heavens. Her

face sparkled with the most incredible brightness. Her eyes looked up to heaven. She was clothed in a brightly radiant robe of white silk and in a cloak decorated with costly jewels: emeralds, sapphires, and pearls both large and small. On her feet she wore shoes made of onyx. But her face was smudged with dust and her dress was torn on the right side. Her cloak, too, had lost its exquisite beauty and the tops of her shoes were soiled. She cried to high heaven with a loud, plaintive voice and said: "Hear me, O heaven, for my countenance is sullied. Mourn, O Earth, for my robe is torn. Tremble, O abyss, for my shoes are soiled. The foxes have their holes and the birds of the sky have their nests, but I have no helper, no consoler, not even a staff to lean on that might give me some support."

And she went on to say: "I was hidden in the heart of the Divine until the Son of Man, conceived and born in virginity, poured out his blood. It was this blood that was his dowry when he married me, so that I might bring forth anew, in the pure and simple rebirth in the Spirit and in water, those who were stunted and sullied by the venom of the serpent. Priests are supposed to be those who nourish me, who see to it that my face sparkles like the morning light, that my robe shines like lightning, that my cloak radiates like costly jewels and that my shoes brightly gleam. But instead they cover my face with dust, tear my robe, and make my cloak dark, and my shoes black. Those who should be beautifying me in every way have been faithless and have totally abandoned me. . . . The wounds of my Bridegroom (Christ) remain fresh and open, so long as the wounds of the human race's sins are open. . . ." And I heard a voice from heaven which said: "This image represents the Church. . . ."

For the full description of this dream-vision, see *Hildegard of Bingen's Book of Divine Works*, pp. 328–31. On the theme of the Bride and the Bridegroom, compare the book of Revelation, 19:7–8, 21:1–2, 9.

11. Compare Steiner's indication that "John" is an occult name for someone who has reached a certain stage of spiritual development, namely, the complete purification of the soul (or, in occult terminology, the transformation of the astral body into the spirit-self [see note 35]) (Oct. 31, 1906, *Kosmogonie*). On another occasion, Steiner states explicitly that Francis of Assisi had a completely purified astral body (July 5, 1906, *Kosmogonie*).

12. Compare *The Little Flowers of St. Francis*, chap. 25 ("How St. Francis Miraculously Healed a Man with Leprosy in Soul and Body").

LECTURE TWO

13. The Vedas ("Veda" = Word, Knowledge) are four collections (Samhitas) of sacred hymns and oblational verses composed in ancient Sanskrit: the Rig Veda, Sama Veda, Yajur Veda, and Atharva Veda. In a broader sense, the Vedas also include the expository texts, the Brahmanas, the Aranyakas, and the Upanishads. The Vedanta ("end of the Vedas") consists primarily of the Upanishads, the Brahma-sutras (commentaries on the Upanishads) and the Bhagavad Gita (part of the epic poem, the Mahabharata). The Vedanta is the basis of Hindu philosophy and religion.

14. On Atlantis, see Steiner: *Cosmic Memory*, chaps. 2-4.

15. The secrets betrayed during the Atlantean age were related to physical reproduction and the formation of races (see Steiner: *Occult Science*, chap. 4, p. 192 ff; and Oct. 7, 1917, *The Fall of the Spirits of Darkness*, lec. 5).

16. Regarding "castes or races," Steiner states that in the first post-Atlantean cultural epoch a social classification existed based on differences in bodily physiognomy and gesture, and that the caste system developed as these physical differences receded (Mar. 23, 1923, *The Driving Force of Spiritual Powers in World History*, lec. 6).

17. The European Mystery Centers in pre-Christian times were those of the Druids in Central Europe and the Trotten in Scandinavia and northern Russia (see Steiner: May 6, 1909, "The European Mysteries and Their Initiates").

18. Compare Steiner's description of the great initiate known as Scythianus: Aug. 31, 1909 (*The East in Light of the West*, lec. 9); and Nov. 14, 1909 (*Die Tieferen Geheimnisse des Menschheitswerdens*).

19. In ancient times the different races fostered different stages in the development of the soul; in the present age this parallelism between the body and the soul has diminished and it will continue to diminish for the remainder of earth evolution (see Steiner: Oct. 7, 1917, *The Fall of the Spirits of Darkness*, lec. 5).

20. Attila: died 453 A.D. King of the Huns from 434-453.

21. Siddhartha Gautama, Gautama Buddha: 563?-483? B.C. Steiner characterizes him as the great teacher of love and compassion (e.g., Sept. 16, 1909, *The Gospel of St. Luke*, lec. 2).

22. Steiner places this school in the seventh and eighth century A.D. (see: Dec. 18, 1912, *Esoteric Christianity and the Mission of Christian Rosenkreutz*, lec. 13; and Dec. 22, 1913, *Between Death and Rebirth*, lec. 5).

23. Saint Paul (born Saul of Tarsus): A.D. 1?-67. Became the foremost Christian Apostle to the Gentiles after experiencing the Risen Christ in the spiritual atmosphere of the earth. (See: Acts of the Apostles, 9:1-9; and Steiner: Oct. 12, 1911, *From Jesus to Christ*, lec. 8.)

24. Clairvoyant observation distinguishes several "higher bodies" in addition to the physical body. The "etheric body" is the body of forces that endows a physical body with life (plants have these two bodies). Animals and human beings have in addition an "astral body" as the basis for their consciousness, and human beings have an "ego-body" as the basis for their self-consciousness. In human development, these bodies are born (become fully independent) at different times: the physical body is developed from birth until age seven (change of teeth), the etheric body is born and developed from age seven to fourteen (puberty), the astral body from age fourteen to twenty-one, and the ego (ego-body) after age twenty-one. (For further details, see Steiner: *Theosophy*, chap. 1; *The Education of the Child in the Light of Anthroposophy*; and Mar. 14, 1910 [misdated 1909], *Metamorphoses of the Soul*, lec. 5.) See also note 35.

25. Compare Steiner's description of a basic law of karma and reincarnation:

> What is present in the astral body in one life [as learning], becomes an attribute of the etheric body in the next life [a habit]. If you meet a person with a certain praiseworthy habit, a habit that repeatedly comes to expression, this indicates that the corresponding concepts were absorbed or developed by this person in the earlier incarnation (Oct. 15, 1906, "Karma and Details of the Law of Karma").

26. At the Crucifixion on Golgotha (Calvary), the macrocosmic Christ Impulse that had lived in Jesus of Nazareth passed into the whole earth. (See Steiner: May 26 & 31, 1908, *The Gospel of*

St. John, lecs. 7 & 12; and Oct. 1, 1911, *The Etherisation of the Blood*, also in *The Reappearance of Christ in the Etheric*, lec. 9.)

Compare here Steiner's description of one of the occult means by which the Christ Impulse is propagated, namely, through a spiritual multiplication of the bodies of Jesus of Nazareth. Steiner states that the astral body of Francis of Assisi was interwoven with a copy of the astral body of Jesus of Nazareth (see: Feb. 15, Mar. 7, Apr. 6 & 11, and May 16, 1909, *The Principle of Spiritual Economy*, lecs. 2, 3, 6, 8 & 9). Note also the close connection between the forces in Jesus of Nazareth's astral body and the spiritual forces of the Buddha (see Steiner's lecture cycle *The Gospel of St. Luke*). Compare also note 11.

27.   Almost nothing is known of the physical ancestry of the Apostles; it is assumed that most of them were from the region of Galilee (Judas was from Judaea). Compare Steiner's comment: "Galilee was the region where peoples of every race and tribe had mixed together. The term Galilean means 'mixed-breed,' 'mongrel'" (May 23, 1908, *The Gospel of St. John*, lec. 5).

28.   Compare St. Paul: "In a word, there are three things that last for ever: faith, hope, and love; but the greatest of them all is love" (1 Cor. 13:13 [New English Bible]).

29.   Plato: 427-347 B.C. On his philosophy of virtue, see especially the *Meno* and the *Republic*.

30.   Plato was connected with the Dionysian Mysteries. (See Frederick Hiebel: *The Gospel of Hellas*, chap. 5; and Steiner: *Christianity as Mystical Fact and the Mysteries of Antiquity*, chap. 4.)

31.   The Greek terms for wisdom, courage, temperance, and justice, are respectively: *sophia, andreia, sophrosyne*, and *dikaiosyne*.

32.   Compare St. Paul: First Corinthians, chapter 13.

LECTURE THREE

33.   On Steiner's conception of evil as a duality, and for examples of karmic compensation, see his lectures of May 1910: *Manifestations of Karma*, esp. lecs. 4-8.

34. Aristotle: 384-322 B.C. On his philosophy of the mean, see the *Nicomachean Ethics* (esp. II.vi-ix) and the *Eudemian Ethics* (esp. II.iii-v); see also St. Thomas Aquinas, *Commentary on the Nicomachean Ethics*, vol. 1, lecs. 6-11, and J. O. Urmson, *Aristotle's Ethics*, chap. 2.

35. The stages in the spiritual evolution of humanity mentioned here by Steiner presuppose an understanding of the full "spiritual anatomy" of the human being. As detailed in Steiner's books *Theosophy* (chap. 1) and *Occult Science* (chap. 2), the complete human being of spirit, soul and body, consists of 3 x 3 members:

spirit:	spirit-human	*Geistmensch*
	life-spirit	*Lebensgeist*
	spirit-self	*Geistselbst*
soul:	consciousness-soul	*Bewusstseinsseele*
	mind-soul	*Verstandesseele*
	(or heart-soul)	(or *Gemütsseele*)
	sentient-soul	*Empfindungsseele*
body:	soul-body	*Seelenleib*
	(or sentient-body)	(or *Empfindungsleib*)
	etheric body	*Aetherleib*
	(or life-body)	(or *Lebensleib*)
	physical body	*Physischer Leib*

In the course of cosmic evolution, through extremely complicated processes, divine-spiritual beings created the threefold human body and the germ of the threefold human spirit, and then brought these together to create an inner realm, the threefold human soul. In particular, part of the soul-body was transformed into the sentient-soul, part of the etheric body into the mind-soul, and part of the physical body into the consciousness-soul. The last of these steps, which represented the transition from a dream-like state of consciousness to the first beginnings of individualized self-consciousness, was achieved by the end of the Atlantean age (cf. note 5). During the subsequent epochs of the post-Atlantean age, human self-consciousness increased as each of the members above the physical body were successively refined as instruments of self-consciousness. This is the temporal sequence Steiner alludes to in the text:

Ancient Indian epoch	etheric body
Ancient Persian epoch	soul-body
Chaldaic–Egyptian epoch	sentient-soul
Greco–Latin epoch	mind-soul
5th epoch (present)	consciousness-soul
6th epoch	spirit-self
7th epoch	life-spirit

In the present (fifth) epoch, humanity has acquired the possibility of full self-consciousness (freedom of thought). Further evolution now depends on the conscious activity of the individual ego. Through the practice of virtue, the individual can bring about the transformation of the threefold body from within: the soul-body becomes transformed into the spirit-self, the etheric body into the life-spirit, and the physical body into the spirit-human. In this way the eternal spirit of the individual comes to manifestation (the higher ego or higher self comes to birth within the lower ego). (See Steiner: *Cosmic Memory*, esp. chap. 17; and his lectures of: Nov. 18, 1907, *Menschheitsentwickelung und Christus-Erkenntnis*, lec. 17; Feb. 29, 1908, *The Influence of Spiritual Beings upon Man*, lec. 4; and May 26 & 30, 1908, *The Gospel of St. John*, lecs. 7 & 11.)

It should be noted that Steiner often treats the human being as a four-membered being consisting of: *physical body*, *etheric body*, *astral body* and *ego*. This is because the spiritual part of the human being at the present stage of evolution has not yet become individualized in most people, and because the soul-body and sentient-soul form a functional unity—traditionally termed the "astral body"—while the mind-soul and consciousness-soul have their unifying center in the ego.

36. The first principle of the Theosophical Society is "to form a nucleus of the Universal Brotherhood of Humanity without distinction of race, creed, sex, caste, or color."

37. See: *The Spiritual Guidance of the Individual and Humanity*, chap. 2.

38. See Steiner's books *Cosmic Memory* and *Occult Science*.

39. Earlier in this lecture, Steiner described *apathy* and *blind passion* as the extremes of *interest*, but also stated that interest was a precondition for any sort of moral action. On the extremes between

which *truthfulness* is the virtuous mean, compare his characteriza-
tion of *truth* as the mean between *error* and *fanaticism* (one-sided
truth) (Oct. 29, 1910, "Der menschliche Charakter").

40.   William Shakespeare: 1564–1616. His tragic drama *The Life of
      Timon of Athens* is believed to have been written between 1606
      and 1609.

41.   Matthew 25:40 (King James Version).

42.   In Book IV of the *Republic* (436 ff.), Plato distinguishes three
      souls—the rational (*logistikon*), the spirited or irascible (*thym-
      oeides*), and the appetitive (*epithymetikon*)—and characterizes
      temperance as the virtue of the appetitive soul when ruled by the
      rational soul (442d). Aristotle characterizes temperance similarly
      (*Nicomachean Ethics*, III.x-xii).

43.   Compare note 36.

44.   Compare Steiner's description of the early Greek conception of
      "justice":

> That which brings about the balance between suffering and happi-
> ness, between goodness and evil is justice. But the Greek genius
> said to itself: when we look out over the world, then we see that
> justice is present to a very limited degree in the world within the
> human ego and astral body. The Greeks experienced the feebleness
> of the human being with respect to justice. Out in nature, however,
> they saw the ceaseless flux, the rising and the setting of the sun, the
> flourishing and fading of the plant world . . . and experienced in
> this a far deeper justice than can be realized by the feeble human
> being. They looked upwards and said to themselves: behind what
> we can see there must exist hidden forces and powers which regu-
> late everything. . . . Although they are hidden, they must be there.
> The Greek genius recognized these and called them the Titans
> because they were not like the feeble human beings; and Themis,
> the Goddess of Justice, is one of the female Titans (Oct. 21, 1910,
> "Die Mission des Zornes").

In other lectures, Steiner indicates that "justice" is specifically
related to the regulation of the physical forces of the human being
(Jan. 15, 1915, "The Great Virtues"; and Aug. 6, 1916, *The Riddle
of Humanity*, lec. 5). In this sense, it is equivalent to the future
virtue of life-wisdom, except that with life-wisdom the individual
will consciously regulate the physical body from within.

45. See, for example, Plato's *Theaetetus* (155D) and Aristotle's *Meta-physics* (I.ii, 982b11).

46. For a more detailed description of the path to the supersensible that begins with wonder, see Steiner: Dec. 27 & 28, 1911 (*The World of the Senses and the World of the Spirit*, lecs. 1 & 2); and Jan. 15, 1912 (*Erfahrungen des Übersinnlichen*, lec. 3).

47. See, for example, Steiner's lectures of: Aug. 25, 1909 (*The East in the Light of the West*, lec. 3); Oct. 25, 1909, & May 2 & 8, 1910 (*The Christ Impulse and the Development of Ego Consciousness*, lecs. 6 & 7); and May 5, 1910 (*Metamorphoses of the Soul*, vol. 2).

It should be noted that for Steiner, true conscience is not just internalized mundane authority, but is rather an inner experience of the higher self (an experience he also calls "moral intuition"). (See: *The Philosophy of Freedom*, chaps. 9 & 12; Aug. 25, 1909, *The East in the Light of the West*, lec. 3; Aug. 20, 1922, *The Evolution of Consciousness*, lec. 2; and Oct. 7, 1922, *The Younger Generation*, lec. 5.)

48. Aeschylus: 525-456 B.C. In his *Oresteia* trilogy (written ca. 458 B.C.), Orestes is pursued by the Erinyes.

Euripides: ca. 484-406 B.C. His last play *Orestes* (written ca. 408 B.C.) treats the same theme as Aeschylus's trilogy, but Orestes is now tormented by his conscience. See Frederick Hiebel, *The Epistles of Paul and Rudolf Steiner's "Philosophy of Free-dom"*, chap. 1.

49. Here Steiner does not give different names to love that is active in outer life (socially) and love that is active inwardly (spiritually). Compare, however, the distinction he makes elsewhere between "love"—the experience of the other in one's own soul—and "devotion" or "self-surrender"—the experience of oneself in the other (*A Road to Self-Knowledge; The Threshold of the Spiritual World*, part 2, chap. 9).

50. Earlier in May 1912, Steiner also listed compassion (brotherly love) as a characteristic that first appeared during the fourth post-Atlantean cultural epoch (May 14, 1912, *Earthly and Cosmic Man*, lec. 6). On the other hand, devotion (cf. previous note) was already

present among the ancient Indians of the first post-Atlantean cultural epoch (see Lecture One).

51. Steiner says here *Lebenskunst* (art of life) instead of *Lebensweisheit* (life-wisdom).

52. Steiner alludes here to a subject that he spoke of frequently between 1910 and 1912:

> That which has hitherto had a justified place in the world as faith, will be replaced by what may be called the Vision of Christ (Oct. 8, 1911, *From Jesus to Christ*, lec. 4).

> Consciousness will build further on the foundation of the forms that compassion and conscience have thus far taken, going on to develop the spiritual vision that was previously attainable only in abnormal states of consciousness. To say this is not to make a prophecy but to state a fact determined by strictly scientific means (May 6, 1912, *Christ in the Twentieth Century*).

> Paralleling the appearance of the Event at Damascus, a great many people will experience something like the following in the course of the twentieth century. As soon as they have acted in some way, they will learn to contemplate their deed. They will become more thoughtful and will have an inner picture of the deed. . . . At first they will not understand it, but those who have studied spiritual science will know that it is not a dream but a picture showing the karmic fulfillment of the act. They will know that one day what is pictured will take place as the fulfillment, the karmic balancing of what was done. . . . What will make it possible for men to see the karmic pictures? It will come as a result of the soul having stood for some time in the light of conscience (May 8, 1910, *The Christ Impulse*, lec. 7).

For further details, see his lectures of: May 31, 1908 (*The Gospel of St. John*, lec. 12); May 28, 1910 (*Manifestations of Karma*, lec. 11); Oct. 7 & 14, 1911 (*From Jesus to Christ*, lecs. 3 & 10); Dec. 2, 1911 (*Faith, Love, Hope*, lec. 1); and Feb. 3, 1912 ("Conscience and Astonishment"). See also the collection of lectures entitled *The Reappearance of Christ in the Etheric*.

53. Although Steiner does not speak here of faith, love, and hope, he did do so at the end of Lecture Two. The forces of hope may be sustained by outwardly acquired knowledge of the teaching of karma and reincarnation (see Steiner's lecture of Dec. 2, 1911,

Faith, Love, Hope, lec. 1), but the ultimate source of this knowledge is true conscience and its future clairvoyant development (cf. notes 47 & 52).

Compare also Steiner's description of hope as the mean between doubt or despair and impatience (Nov. 3, 1910, *The Wisdom of Man, of the Soul, and of the Spirit*, lec. 7).

54. Compare Steiner:

> After the baptism by John in the Jordan river, when the ego of Jesus of Nazareth left the three bodies, the human organism that stood there contained in full consciousness that Higher Self of humanity which otherwise works with cosmic wisdom on a child without its knowledge [during its first three years] (*The Spiritual Guidance of the Individual and Humanity*, chap. 1).

> In respect of the earthly life of Christ, ... [the Baptism] was something like conception in the case of a human being. And we understand the life of Christ from then onwards until the Mystery of Golgotha when we compare it with the life of the human embryo within the body of the mother. From the Baptism by John until the Mystery of Golgotha, therefore, the Christ Being passes through a kind of embryonic existence. The Mystery of Golgotha itself is to be understood as the earthly birth—that is to say, the death of Jesus is to be understood as the earthly birth of the Christ (Oct. 3, 1913, *The Fifth Gospel*, lec. 3).

On the subsequent resurrection of Jesus and his continuing union with the Christ, see Steiner's lectures of: July 7, 1909 (*The Gospel of St. John and Its Relation to the Other Gospels*, lec. 1); and Jan. 1, 1913 (*The Bhagavad-Gita and the Epistles of Paul*, lec. 5).

55. Regarding the "unclothed" Christ Impulse, compare Steiner's interpretation of the passage in St. Mark's Gospel where Jesus is taken captive in the Garden of Gethsemane: "Among those following was a young man with nothing on but a linen cloth. They tried to seize him; but he slipped out of the linen cloth and ran away naked" (Mark 14:51-52 [NEB]). Steiner indicates that this youth represents "the youthful cosmic Christ Impulse," the "'seed' of a new world order," who slips away and then reappears after the Resurrection as the youth at the sepulcher (Mark 16:1-6). (See Steiner: Sept. 23, 1912, *The Gospel of St. Mark*, lec. 9; and Apr. 10, 1917,

Building Stones for an Understanding of the Mystery of Golgotha, lec. 3. See also Oskar Kürten: "The Son of Man and the Cosmic Christ.")

On the "first human being" and the "last human being," compare St. Paul on the "first Adam" and the "last Adam" (1 Cor. 15:45-49). See also Steiner: June 26, 1908 (*The Apocalypse of St. John,* lec. 9); and Oct. 10, 1911 (*From Jesus to Christ,* lec. 6).

56. Compare Steiner's indication that the forces of faith, love, and hope bring about the transformation of the astral body, etheric body, and physical body respectively into the spirit-self, life-spirit, and spirit-human (cf. note 35) (June 14, 1911, "Faith, Love and Hope").

Compare also Steiner's remark in a letter to his future wife Marie von Sivers: "The 'being' of Christ should be thought of as the inverse macrocosmic human being, but identical with the second aspect of the Divinity, the Logos" (Jan. 13, 1906, *Correspondence and Documents,* p. 83). On the relation of the human being to the Christ being, see Steiner's lecture of Jan. 9, 1912, *Cosmic Ego and Human Ego.*

57. Johann Wolfgang von Goethe: 1749–1832. German poet, playwright, scientist and statesman. Karl August, Duke of Sachsen-Weimar-Eisenach (1757–1828), was Goethe's friend and sponsor after 1775. The quotation is from a letter to Friedrich August von Beulitz, July 18, 1828.

References

Note: Works of Rudolf Steiner are keyed to the volumes in the *Rudolf Steiner Gesamtausgabe* (abbreviated "GA"), the complete edition of Rudolf Steiner's works published in German by the Rudolf Steiner Verlag, Dornach, Switzerland.

Aquinas, Thomas. *Commentary on the Nicomachean Ethics*. Translated by C. I. Litzinger. Chicago: Henry Regnery Co., 1964.

Aristotle. *Aristotle's Eudemian Ethics: Books I, II, and VIII*. Translated by Michael Woods. Oxford: Clarendon Press, 1982.

——. "Metaphysics." In *The Basic Works of Aristotle*. Edited by Richard McKeon. New York: Random House, 1941.

——. "Nicomachean Ethics." In *The Basic Works of Aristotle*. Edited by Richard McKeon. New York: Random House, 1941.

Francis of Assisi. *The Little Flowers of St. Francis*. Translated by Raphael Brown. Garden City, N.Y.: Hanover House, 1958.

Goethe, Johann Wolfgang von. Letter to Friedrich August von Beulitz. July 18, 1828. In *Goethes Werke: Hg. im Auftrage der Grossherzogin Sophie von Sachsen*. Sect. 4: Letters, vol. 44, p. 210. Weimar 1909.

Hiebel, Frederick. *The Gospel of Hellas*. New York: Anthroposophic Press, 1949.

——. *The Epistles of Paul and Rudolf Steiner's "Philosophy of Freedom"*. Spring Valley, N.Y.: St. George Publ., 1980.

Hildegard of Bingen's Book of Divine Works, with Letters and Songs. Edited by Matthew Fox. Sante Fe: Bear & Co., 1987.

Kürten, Oskar. "The Son of Man and the Cosmic Christ." *Newsletter of the Anthroposophical Society in America*, Spring 1985, pp. 2–4.

Plato. "Meno." In *The Collected Dialogues of Plato Including the Letters.* Edited by Edith Hamilton and Huntington Cairns. New York: Pantheon Books, 1961.

———. "Republic." In *The Collected Dialogues of Plato Including the Letters.* Edited by Edith Hamilton and Huntington Cairns. New York: Pantheon Books, 1961.

———. "Theaetetus." In *The Collected Dialogues of Plato Including the Letters.* Edited by Edith Hamilton and Huntington Cairns. New York: Pantheon Books, 1961.

Schopenhauer, Arthur. "Preisschrift über die Grundlagen der Moral." In *Sämtliche Werke,* vol. 7, p. 133. Stuttgart: Cotta'sche Buchhandlung, 1894.

Steiner, Rudolf. *The Apocalypse of St. John.* Translated by Johanna Collis. London: Rudolf Steiner Press, 1977. (GA 104)

———. *Between Death and Rebirth.* Translated by E. H. Goddard and D. S. Osmond. London: Rudolf Steiner Press, 1975. (GA 141)

———. *The Bhagavad-Gita and the Epistles of Paul.* Translated by Lisa D. Monges and Doris M. Bugbey. Spring Valley, N.Y.: Anthroposophic Press, 1971. (GA 142)

———. *Building Stones for an Understanding of the Mystery of Golgotha.* Translated by A. H. Parker. London: Rudolf Steiner Press, 1972. (GA 175)

———. *The Christ Impulse and the Development of Ego Consciousness.* Translated by Lisa D. Monges and Gilbert Church. Spring Valley, N.Y.: Anthroposophic Press, 1976. (GA 116)

———. *Christ in the Twentieth Century.* Translated by Marjorie Spock. Spring Valley, N.Y.: Anthroposophic Press, 1971. (GA 69)

———. *Christianity as Mystical Fact and the Mysteries of Antiquity.* Translated by E. A. Frommer, Gabrielle Hess, and Peter Kändler. Blauvelt, N.Y.: Steinerbooks, 1961. (GA 8)

———. "Conscience and Astonishment." Translator unknown. *The Golden Blade*, 1967, pp. 5–18. (GA 143)

———. *Correspondence and Documents*. Translated by Christian and Ingrid von Arnim. London: Rudolf Steiner Press & New York: Anthroposophic Press, 1988. (GA 262)

———. *Cosmic Ego and Human Ego*. Translated by Frances E. Dawson. New York: Anthroposophic Press, 1941. (GA 130)

———. *Cosmic Memory: Prehistory of Earth and Man*. Translated by Karl E. Zimmer. San Francisco: Harper & Row, 1959. (GA 11)

———. *The Driving Force of Spiritual Powers in World History*. Translated by Dorothy Osmond and Johanna Collis. N. Vancouver, B. C.: Steiner Book Centre, 1972. (GA 222)

———. *Earthly and Cosmic Man*. Translated by D. S. Osmond. London: Rudolf Steiner Press, 1948. (GA 133)

———. *The East in Light of the West*. Translator unknown. London: Rudolf Steiner Press & New York: Anthroposophic Press, 1940. (GA 113)

———. *The Education of the Child in the Light of Anthroposophy*. Translated by Mary and George Adams. London: Rudolf Steiner Press, 1975. (GA 34)

———. *Erfahrungen des Übersinnlichen*. Dornach: Rudolf Steiner Verlag, 1994. (GA 143)

———. *Esoteric Christianity and the Mission of Christian Rosenkreutz*. Translated by Pauline Wehrle. London: Rudolf Steiner Press, 1984. (GA 130)

———. *The Etherisation of the Blood*. Translated by Arnold Freeman and D. S. Osmond. London: Rudolf Steiner Press, 1971. (GA 130)

———. "The European Mysteries and Their Initiates." Translator unknown. *Anthroposophical Quarterly*, 1964, no. 1, pp. 170–76. (GA 57)

——. *The Evolution of Consciousness.* Translated by V. E. Watkin and C. Davy. London: Rudolf Steiner Press, 1979. (GA 227)

——. "Faith, Love and Hope." Translator unknown. *Anthroposophical News Sheet*, October 26, 1947, no. 41–42, pp.161–63. (GA 127)

——. *Faith, Love, Hope.* Translated by Violet Watkin. N. Vancouver, B.C.: Steiner Book Centre n.d. (GA 130)

——. *The Fall of the Spirits of Darkness.* Translated by Anna Meuss. Bristol: Rudolf Steiner Press, 1993. (GA 177)

——. *The Fifth Gospel.* Translated by C. Davy and D. S. Osmond. London: Rudolf Steiner Press, 1968. (GA 148)

——. *From Jesus to Christ.* Translated by H. Collison and C. D[avy]. London: Rudolf Steiner Press, 1973. (GA 131)

——. *The Gospel of St. John.* Translated by Maud B. Monges. Spring Valley, N.Y.: Anthroposophic Press, 1962. (GA 103)

——. *The Gospel of St. John and Its Relation to the Other Gospels.* Translated by Samuel Lockwood, Loni Lockwood, and Maria St. Goar, edited by Stewart C. Easton. Spring Valley, N.Y.: Anthroposophic Press, 1982. (GA 112)

——. *The Gospel of St. Luke.* Translated by D. S. Osmond and Owen Barfield. London: Rudolf Steiner Press, 1964. (GA 114)

——. *The Gospel of St. Mark.* Translated by Conrad Mainzer, edited by Stewart C. Easton. Hudson, N.Y.: Anthroposophic Press & London: Rudolf Steiner Press, 1986. (GA 139)

——. "The Great Virtues." Translator unknown. *The Golden Blade,* 1969, pp. 5–21. (GA 159)

——. *The Influence of Spiritual Beings Upon Man.* Translator unknown. Spring Valley, N.Y.: Anthroposophic Press, 1961. (GA 102)

——. "Karma and Details of the Law of Karma." Translated by D. S. Osmond. *Anthroposophical Quarterly*, 1978, no. 1, pp. 2–8. (GA 127)

——. *Kosmogonie*. Dornach, Switzerland: Rudolf Steiner Verlag, 1979. (GA 94)

——. *Manifestations of Karma*. Translator unknown. London: Rudolf Steiner Press, 1984. (GA 120)

——. *Menschheitsentwickelung und Christus-Erkenntnis*. Dornach, Switzerland: Rudolf Steiner Verlag, 1967. (GA 100)

——. "Der menschliche Charakter." *Beiträge zur Rudolf Steiner Gesamtausgabe*, no. 81 (Michaeli 1983), pp. 26–39.

——. *Metamorphoses of the Soul.* Translated by C. Davy and C. von Arnim. London: Rudolf Steiner Press, 1983, vol. 1 & 2. (GA 58 & 59)

——. "Die Mission des Zornes." *Beiträge zur Rudolf Steiner Gesamtausgabe*, no. 81 (Michaeli 1983), pp. 7–25.

——. *Occult Science: An Outline*. Translated by George and Mary Adams. London: Rudolf Steiner Press, 1979. (GA 13)

——. *The Philosophy of Freedom*. Translated by Michael Wilson. London: Rudolf Steiner Press, 1988. (GA 4)

——. *The Principle of Spiritual Economy*. Translated by Peter Mollenhauer. Hudson, N.Y.: Anthroposophic Press & London: Rudolf Steiner Press, 1986. (GA 109)

——. *The Reappearance of Christ in the Etheric*. Edited by Gilbert Church and Alice Wulsin. Spring Valley, N.Y.: Anthroposophic Press, 1983. (GA 118, 130, 178 & 182)

——. *The Riddle of Humanity*. Translated by John F. Logan. London: Rudolf Steiner Press, 1990. (GA 170)

——. *A Road to Self-Knowledge; The Threshold of the Spiritual World*. Translated by M. Cotterell. London: Rudolf Steiner Press, 1975. (GA 16 & 17)

——. *The Spiritual Guidance of the Individual and Humanity*. Translated by Samuel Desch. Hudson, N.Y.: Anthroposophic Press, 1992. (GA 15)

———. *Theosophy: An Introduction to the Spiritual Processes in Human Life and in the Cosmos.* Translated by Catherine E. Creeger. Hudson, N.Y.: Anthroposophic Press, 1993. (GA 9)

———. *Die Tieferen Geheimnisse des Menschheitswerdens.* Dornach, Switzerland: Rudolf Steiner Verlag, 1966. (GA 117)

———. *The Wisdom of Man, of the Soul, and of the Spirit: Anthroposophy, Psychosophy, Pneumatosophy.* Translated by Samuel and Loni Lockwood. New York: Anthroposophic Press, 1971. (GA 115)

———. *The World of the Senses and the World of the Spirit.* Translator unknown. London: Rudolf Steiner Press, 1947. (GA 134)

———. *The Younger Generation.* Translated by R. M. Querido. Spring Valley, N.Y.: Anthroposophic Press, 1967. (GA 217)

Urmson, J. O. *Aristotle's Ethics.* Oxford: Basil Blackwell, 1988.

Voragine, Jacobus de. *The Golden Legend of Jacobus de Voragine.* Translated by Granger Ryan and Helmut Ripperger. New York: Arno Press, 1969.

DURING THE LAST TWO DECADES of the nineteenth century, the Austrian-born Rudolf Steiner (1861–1925) became a respected and well-published scientific, literary, and philosophical scholar, particularly known for his work on Goethe's scientific writings. After the turn of the century he began to develop his earlier philosophical principles into an approach to methodical research of psychological and spiritual phenomena.

His multifaceted genius has led to innovative and holistic approaches in medicine, science, education (Waldorf schools), special education, philosophy, religion, economics, agriculture (Biodynamic method), architecture, drama, new arts of eurythmy and speech, and other fields. In 1924 he founded the General Anthroposophical Society, which today has branches throughout the world.

*For an informative catalog of the work of Rudolf Steiner
and other anthroposophical authors please contact*

ANTHROPOSOPHIC PRESS
RR 4 Box 94 A-1 Hudson, NY 12534
TEL: 518 851 2054
FAX: 518 851 2047